BOB GARRATT is Chairman of Media Projects
International in London and of Organization
Development Limited in Hong Kong. He has a glob-
al consultancy advising on corporate governance,
director development and strategic thinking. He is a
founder member of the Task Force to create the
·Commonwealth Association for Corporate
Governance. He is visiting professor in Corporate
Governance at the Imperial College of Science,
Technology and Medicine, London and a Senior
Associate of the Judge Institute of Management,
University of Cambridge. His previous titles include
*Learning to Lead, Developing Strategic Thought* of
which he is editor, *The Fish Rots from the Head* and
*The Twelve Organizational Capabilities.*

D1642829

# The Learning Organization

*Developing Democracy at Work*

## BOB GARRATT

**HarperCollinsBusiness**
*An Imprint of HarperCollinsPublishers*

An Imprint of HarperCollins*Publishers*
77–85 Fulham Palace Road,
Hammersmith, London W6 8JB

www.fireandwater.com/business

Published by HarperCollins*Publishers* 2001
9 8 7 6 5 4 3 2 1

First published in Great Britain by
HarperCollinsPublishers 2000

Copyright © Bob Garratt 2000

The Author asserts the moral right to be
identified as the author of this work

ISBN 0 00 653053 2

Set in Sabon and Rotis Semi Serif by
Rowland Phototypesetting Ltd,
Bury St Edmunds, Suffolk

Printed and bound in Great Britain by
Omnia Books Limited, Glasgow

To Michael Lloyd, Alvin Boyarsky and Reg Revans –
the three mentors who delegated sufficient authority
for me to make the mistakes by which to learn

and to the friend and tutor who kept me learning
when the distractions were many – Beverly Bernstein

# Contents

# Introduction

This book argues that organizations can only become simultaneously effective and efficient if there is conscious and continuous learning between three distinct groups – the leaders who direct the enterprise, the staff who deliver the product or service, and the customers or consumers. Opening up such learning processes releases information and energy in ways that demand and encourage more democratic organizational structures and processes. Unless directors, staff and customers are linked through conscious learning on a regular and rigorous basis, the enterprise will die – its rate of learning is outpaced by the rate of change in its external environment and so it fails.

When I first wrote about the Learning Organization in 1986, 'learning' was not an issue for corporate nor national debate. This was well before the notion that the twenty-first century would be about 'the knowledge economy' based on the acquisition of learning to create tangible assets, or 'intellectual property' and mutually supportive networks. Indeed in those days the legal term for intellectual property was 'intangible assets'. In the intervening years learning has become a public issue and the national and corporate views of learning have changed dramatically:

*Learning is the most powerful, engaging, rewarding and enjoyable aspect of our personal and collective experience.*
*The ability to learn about learning and develop the learning process is the critical issue of the twenty-first century.*
*Learning has a moral dimension.*
*The capacity to learn is an asset which never becomes obsolete.*
*Individual and collective learning reinforces the informed, conscious and discriminating choices that underpin democracy.*

This selection of five quotes from *A Declaration On Learning* (1998)[1] shows a range of the issues now being discussed in public. The aspiration to become a 'Learning Organization' is now common enough to form part of many annual company statements, although this is often treated as cynically by their staff as the old mantra of 'our people are our biggest asset'. There is still a long way to go before the right (and the duty) to learn is accepted by bosses and politicians alike as a basic human right. In part this is because opening up learning, and the consequent critical review of current organizational structures and practices, often reflects badly on those currently in power. All learning has a moral dimension, not all of which is good. Yet in a fast-changing world the pressure is always on those very leaders to ensure that the rate of the organization's learning is equal to, or greater than, the rate of environmental change.

Peter Senge's publication of *The Fifth Discipline* in the early 1990s put much impetus behind the Learning Organization idea. However, his book deals essentially with systems thinking and plays down the social-emotional aspects and the political consequences of learning. I have tried to rebalance the organizational learning equation in this book.

I still have plenty of telephone calls from executives who 'want a Learning Organization quickly'. They get a short answer from me. The Learning Organization is more of a continuing aspiration than a product. I explain to such callers that I have never met a truly 'Learning Organization'. Yet it is an idea which certainly stretches and motivates people and organizations for the long haul to achieve their vision. The Chinese have classical paintings of the five-clawed Dragon Emperor forever stretching out to grasp the ever-elusive flaming pink pearl of knowledge. He never reaches it. But he never stops trying. I see Learning Organizations like that.

Henry Mintzberg in *The Strategy Safari*[2] suggests that the idea of organizational learning is both the biggest breakthrough in business and management thinking of the last few decades and is, most importantly, sustainable. I argue that the development of conscious organizational learning is crucial to the survival and development of our enterprises and of our civil society. It is not another management fad that leads to organizational bulimia where executives binge on it for a year or two, get bored, throw up and then try something else.

A reflective person might ask 'why is such a focus necessary? Surely, all organizations must learn or they die?' This is correct. But many under-performing organizations take a long time to die and the time lapse between them shutting off their sources of information and their demise is often long, painful, and socially and environmentally destructive. There is an inertia in many organizations which outsiders find hard to understand. Indeed the organizational 'brain' may have been clinically dead for years but the organizational life-support system just keeps things going until someone, usually a banker, throws the off switch.

Coming into business from a background of architecture and design – disciplines based on developing holistic perspectives and being courageous in understanding and tackling often contradictory multidisciplinary needs and then integrating them into a solution – I was surprised at the prevailing technical/accounting and convergent perspectives of directors and senior managers. They tended to focus on a specific problem, regardless of its context, and to fix it as rapidly and short-sightedly as possible. That this would create many other problems due to their non-consideration of either other connections or the context in which the issue was set was not seen as their responsibility. The cumulative consequence was that many organizations degenerated into a series of single-discipline baronies who fought each other over the allocation of scarce resources and who blamed each other when things went wrong. Integrative learning was seen as being for wimps.

As I had a liberal education – which encouraged looking at the biggest possible picture, valuing ideas and divergent thoughts before focusing on finding an elegant solution to complex problems – I seemed like a fish out of water in 1970s management circles. The vast majority of directors and managers with whom I worked seemed content to put the minimum effort into finding the easiest solution and enjoyed quick fixes. They had a need for certainty in a very uncertain world, and an impulse to action rather than to reflection and learning. They judged it better to be seen taking any action rather than be accused of wasting time by thinking reflectively. This often led to habit-forming, action-fixated, behaviour and so blocked their, and the organization's, chances of learning.

Indeed there was often strong resistance to taking time to think and learn as part of these directors' and managers' normal work. The belief that 'we're paid to do things around here, not to think' was worn as a badge of honour in many companies in many countries. It was seen as 'soft' to admit to learning anything as this meant that you did not know everything already. Omniscience was also assumed by the staff of their directors and senior executives. Yet in most of my client organizations there was a constant feeling of vulnerability that as a manager or professional with typically only a single discipline, you would be found lacking when trying to understand other disciplines.

This feeling was reinforced by the different technical languages that other directors and managers used, often to baffle the opposition. It was felt most strongly by the directors who tended to cling to their functional job title, e.g. Finance Director, rather than accept that being a director is about competence *across* an organization rather than within a single area of responsibility. The idea of a director having to manage and transcend the boundaries between specialisms was therefore daunting. The idea of learning to take a 'generalist' view of the organization and its place in the changing world was seen as a wild and impossible ideal well beyond the capacity of a 'normal' director. There was little interest in, or awareness of, the outside world and its changing meaning for the survival of the organization. Politics and international affairs were seen as far beyond most directors' and senior executives' concerns.

Such thinking is beginning to change. The Institute of Directors, London, launched a tough new professional qualification – *The Chartered Director* in 1999[3] – as a measure of a director's understanding of the integrative nature of their work – of truly giving direction and leadership to their organization. Within its syllabus is a compulsory module called *Organizing for Tomorrow* and within that there are sections on *The Learning Organization* and *The Learning Board*. As many thousands of people have applied for training as Chartered Directors since its launch we should begin to see over the next decades a welcome and significant change of mindset in the competences of direction-givers, and in the importance of organizational learning.

But this approach is currently exceptional and much managerial and business thinking is still locked into the application of only 'hard' knowledge and unemotional, analytical/quantitative methods which consciously exclude the importance of people and their learning in their organizations. This is very odd because if we are moving into a 'knowledge economy' in the twenty-first century, then we are using a redundant managerial mindset by focusing only on the inanimate and rational. To quote Max Boisot 'in the "knowledge economy" people are their own tools'.[4] This radical statement takes some digesting. It is crucial to understanding the importance of the Learning Organization, for the development of our societies, and to grasp the need for more democratic organizational structures and processes to ensure that future. Considering the value of people's learning as an asset (rather than as a training cost) will be a necessary and truly major change of managerial mindset.

Most directors are still stuck firmly in the mindsets and selection procedures of the 1970s and 1980s where the single functional specialists rule. This thinking can work well at the start of a professional or managerial career. Once one has to integrate thinking and action *horizontally* between departments in managerial life, and integrate directorial thinking and actions both within and outside the enterprise, such functionally-based criteria collapse. The thinking and learning competences needed to take a 'helicopter view' of the organization are missing. Indeed a substantial part of the broader learning needed to cope with such growing demands as 'the triple bottom-line' – of simultaneous assessment on financial, environmental, and societal performance[5] – is also missing. There is a need for a corporate equivalent of what Oxford University calls a 'PPE' – a philosophy, politics and economics degree – approach for such people to broaden their horizons sufficiently to be competent at direction-giving. Otherwise they are educationally and culturally deprived at a time when such learning is crucial to their, and their organization's, survival.

I was first made aware of this lack in 1975 when I was working as a learning consultant on a series of live-project, action learning programmes for the potential top managers of a major electronics group. One project concerned the development of a radical new communication system which began to integrate telephones with computers. It was a joint project between client and manufacturer and all agreed that the future of British telecommunications hung on the outcome. As the project developed it became obvious that the top managers involved on both sides were still thinking along the lines of enhancing the existing 'copper wire' telephone system and bolting a computer on the end. However, younger project workers saw things very differently and started sending messages to their bosses that this seemed a flawed way of thinking. The potential top managers saw the telephone system as the easy part. The difficult part was to understand the nature of the computing that would become the enabling technology to drive the new products. In this they were weak. Moreover, they realized that this weakness could wreck the project as they would have to compete with existing computer manufacturers who were more advanced than them, and who could easily buy existing telephone experience.

They asked their bosses to reconsider the whole strategy and to link up with computer manufacturers to develop a new integrated technology. The matter was eventually raised at a meeting of all concerned with the project. The chief executive of the project became very angry and attacked the project participants 'for thinking'. He said, 'I do not pay my managers to think, but to do. If they are going to think, then they will do it in their own time on a Sunday.' This was received in shocked silence. It led to great despair in the project team, its slow break-up through the loss of talented potential leaders, and eventually the production of a technically advanced piece of equipment which was so over-specified that the export market did not want it and which the computer producers later leapfrogged with more market-friendly examples. The top managers had set up a brainless, unthinking machine as the project organization and ensured that it was unconnected to the changing needs of the outside world. I knew then that there were many ideas, models, and techniques which could have been applied to help such teams should they wish to think and learn consciously, and I set out to do so. This book is a review of my learning so far.

Today I am delighted that companies such as BP Amoco, Unipart, General Electric, Xerox, Conoco, Analog Devices, Harley-Davidson, Chaparral Steel, British Airways, Jaguar Cars and Rover Group have developed their approaches towards creating Learning Organizations. A noticeable feature of their attempts is the desire to develop regular and rigorous organizational learning flows both within the company and with customers.

Delegating more power to customer-facing staff (often some of the lowest paid employees in an organization) to ensure their development of service quality, and to get rapid feedback of customers' changing needs, represents a major shift in the traditional 'hierarchical position' of power. This is a sign of a gradual democratization process in organizations. Indeed, the growth of many more self-managing groups, and the renaissance of first-line managers with some discretionary authority, are both signs of such a power shift being significant for the future structure and more democratic social processes of our organizations. The growth of information management systems, particularly e-mail and the Internet, has combined with this power shift to make managerial work less concerned with physical supervision and more with systems installation, maintenance and *learning* at the operational level.

Constant economic pressure has decimated managerial jobs over the last two decades. In the short term this has often proved cost effective but many organizations are now finding that after just two or three years there is a longer-term cost to pay. They have also thrown out their experience base – the corporate memory – with those managers and workers; leaving a less capable organization at a time when growing organizational adaptiveness is needed. 'Down-sizing' and 'right-sizing' are leading in many cases to organizational capsizing when over-rationalist accountants and managers are left to their own devices. Then the rate of learning drops below the rate of environmental change and the immediate cost benefits are lost as the customers leave, the cashflow dries up, and the organization goes belly up.

As the day-to-day operational learning part of an organization becomes more self-managing, so the direction-givers are feeling ever more exposed and in search of new roles and tasks. Public outcries are growing fast against the cavalier, and sometimes corrupt, behaviour of some directors and senior executives across the world – whether in, for example, the US, UK, France, Germany, Hong Kong, China, south-east Asia, Africa, or South America. The scandals surrounding The Savings and Loans, Apple Computers, Robert Maxwell, Barings Bank, Metallgesellschaft, Credit Lyonnais, and BCCI are amongst the many cases where a lack of directorial awareness and competence in their duty of holding the enterprise in trust for the future has been shown.

The economic and social case for increasing directorial competence is now well-established as recent reports in the UK, South Africa, France, The Netherlands, Australia and Canada show. What is only just becoming clear is the relationship between directorial competence, business performance and *learning*. Conscious learning has now become both a highly beneficial process for any organization and a tradable asset. Generating and selling know-how and know-why is becoming a core competence of many modern corporations. However, we are still refining our competences of organizational learning at the day-to-day, operational level. When we add these to the newly espoused leadership competences of formulating purpose, vision and values, developing strategic thinking skills, more effective risk-assessment, and greater clarity about accountability, then a powerful vision of the twenty-first-century organization emerges.

The twenty-first-century organization is driven by regular and rigorous learning, particularly through open and critical review and debate, at all levels of the organization, continuously as part of its normal work. By so doing it reinforces and develops the democratic forces for informed choice in our organizations and so strengthens our civil society. Thomas Jefferson said that 'the price of liberty is eternal vigilance'. The Learning Organization adds greatly to that vigilance.

# CHAPTER 1

# Does Organizational Learning Matter?

The simplest answer to the question 'does organizational learning matter?' is 'yes'. Unless an organization can cope with its rapidly changing external environment it will die. Who is ultimately responsible for ensuring a sufficient rate of learning in the organization? There is only one answer legally and practically – the board of directors. In the majority of jurisdictions around the world directors are charged legally with holding the organization in trust for future generations and are, therefore, ultimately accountable for ensuring a sufficient rate of learning throughout their organization, and for creating the emotional climate in which all their people can learn continuously. The executives and managers are then responsible for designing, installing and maintaining the systems (especially of learning) which create the positive emotional climate in which people go about their day-to-day work. How directors and managers ensure that this rate of learning is sufficient is the great challenge for creating and sustaining Learning Organizations – particularly as many do not even recognize that there is a challenge.

My interest is in creating organizational learning systems which balance continuously the triple, interactive loops of Policy (customer-focused), Strategic (director-focused) and Operational (staff-focused) learning to allow the critical review of all levels of the organization; and to capture and evaluate at all three levels the attitudes, knowledge, skills, values and collective memories of their organizations – their cumulative learning. But before we get into the details I think it wise to define our terms.

'Learning' is an ancient and interesting word. It means the

accumulation of, reflection upon, and use of the complex attitudes, knowledge and skills by which an individual or group acquires the ability to actively adapt to their changing environments. In Revans' terms mentioned below, an organization's rate of learning should be equal to, or greater than, the rate of change in their environment[6]:

$$L \geq C$$

Continuous learning is about sensing and responding to the changes in the external and internal worlds of the organization to ensure the survival and development of the energy niches which support it. It is both a holistic and ecological idea.

Continuous learning implies, therefore, much more than the formal, accredited, education systems which most of us still refer to, wrongly, as 'learning'. A recent UK government report on education stated that 'most people stop learning after they leave school'. This is patent nonsense. It may be true that the majority of people do not undertake any formal education and accreditation after they leave school. But they most certainly do not stop continuously learning. Most learning is personal, private, uncodified, hidden and often a defensive way of coping with the effects of a seemingly non-learning employer. I use 'learning' in its active, holistic form in this book.

The earliest reference to 'learning' that I can find is in Durham Cathedral, as part of an eighth-century quotation from Saint Cuthbert. 'Learning' is derived from the old Northumbrian active verb 'leornung', originating from a Germanic root. As early as the seventh century AD St Cuthbert was using the word in its modern, integrative meaning in his writings on Holy Island. Curiously, in non-English languages, particularly the Latin and Chinese-derived languages, the word tends not to have the active, personal and holistic meaning found in English, and so often reflects only the idea of passive, teacher-orientated, and instruction-only 'education'.

## THE THREE LEVELS OF ORGANIZATIONAL LEARNING

The fifteen years since I first wrote about the Learning Organization have reinforced in me two fundamental views of organizational, as distinct from individual, learning. First, that there are three levels of conscious and interactive learning processes necessary to create any effective and efficient human organization:

1. Policy Learning
2. Strategic Learning
3. Operational Learning

which interact in complex and often unpredictable ways.

Second, that there is a growing business case, and public service delivery case, for treating learning as *the* key renewable and sustainable asset. The outputs of organizational 'learning' are seen increasingly as balance sheet items showing the return on the investment in people and their learning by the organization. They are, therefore, treated increasingly as an *asset* linked closely with consciously increasing organizational effectiveness. On the other hand 'training' is seen increasingly as a direct *cost* – a profit and loss account item that ensures continuing operational competence and increased organizational efficiency. Training is necessary but not sufficient; only systems of conscious learning can create a Learning Organization.

The theory that sustainable Learning Organizations consist of three continuous and interacting levels of organizational learning grew directly from Reg Revans' fifty years of research work. His early notions of the interactions between his systems 'Alpha, Beta and Gamma' caused me to reflect and experiment a great deal with the processes of organizational learning.

I concluded that in effective Learning Organizations there is an awareness of the crucial need to strike a continuous balance, through feedback systems, between the external world in which the organization, and the customers or consumers, exist – *Policy Learning* – and the internal world where products are designed and produced, and services delivered by the staff – *Operational Learning*. Put in more business-like terms, it is crucial in Learning Organizations that 'organizational effectiveness' as perceived by the customer is paramount. It needs to be made a priority by every organization and not overshadowed by the natural inclination to overdo 'organizational efficiency'.

The balancing mechanism between Policy and Operational Learning is the central processor of the total organization's learning – *Strategic Learning* – focused by, but not exclusive to, the board of directors. In a Learning Organization the board is at the *centre* of the company – not at the top as it would be in a traditional, hierarchical organization. The board deploys their resources through risk assessments, dilemma resolution and strategic decisions to ensure a balance between 'organizational effectiveness' and 'organizational efficiency'. This is the basis of my *Learning Board* model[7], set within the total learning process of the Learning Organization – those triple loops of learning.

In future chapters I will deal with each level of organizational learning in more detail. But I want to stress here the importance of the often overlooked area of Policy Learning and its relationship with Operational and Strategic Learning. Without understanding this organizations can never act effectively.

## Policy Learning

I define the organization's relationship with the external world – Policy Learning – as the focus of 'organizational effectiveness'. At its simplest, I argue that the customer's or consumer's perception of an organization's effectiveness makes or breaks that organization. It is well-proven, especially through the long-term PIMS[8] studies, that the customer's *perception* of organizational effectiveness has two major benefits. First, a satisfied customer is more likely to make repeat purchases and hence reduce the cost of sales. So a repeat customer is more likely to be a profitable customer at the very least in cost-reduction terms. Second, a satisfied repeat customer is more likely to pay a small price premium as they believe that the product or service is good value for money. A repeat customer who pays a premium is likely to be a profitable

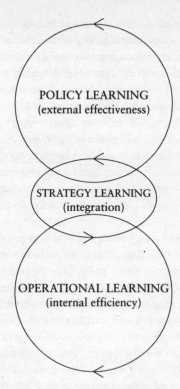

**Figure 1 The Learning Organization Model**

customer – the goal of all businesses. Satisfied repeat customers are also more likely to tell others about your product or service. This happy coincidence of customer loyalty bringing improved margins both through a reduction in the cost of sales and the willingness to pay a price premium is totally dependent on the customer's *perception* – his or her ability to rationalize the use of the product or service, and to value the emotional attachments of so doing. Successful brands are built on these two foundations. Thus any system for continuously reinforcing the customer's perception through the Policy Learning cycle is likely to pay big dividends. This is as true in the public or parastatal sectors where consumer dissatisfaction with perceived organizational ineffectiveness can cause major political problems for governments.

At a more complex level, Policy Learning is about directors, managers and staff combining to make sense of the patterns in the turbulent and fast-changing external environment which provides the macro-political dynamics – the 'energy niches' – in which the organization survives and thrives. Systematic awareness of, and reflection, action, and feedback on, changes in the political, physical, economic, social, technological and trade environments (often called the 'PPESTT analysis') allow a board to create its 'political will' in relation to this changing environment – to give effective direction and leadership to achieve its purpose. Such clarity gives everyone in the organization the chance of contributing to create a sustainable advantage in Policy Learning over its competitors.

Notice that there has been a shift of organizational power in what I have advocated. Everyone can now help monitor and reflect on the changes in customer needs. This should no longer be the special domain of the board, or the marketing department, alone. The board is ultimately accountable for driving the enterprise forward and keeping it under control. But in a Learning Organization the board of directors accepts that it is not omniscient and has many things to learn from its 'customer-facing' staff.

Policy Learning cannot be handled in isolation – it is part of the infinite game of total organizational learning. As a brief example of the interaction with the other two levels of strategy and operations, let me outline what can then happen.

## Operational Learning

Encouraging learning in the 'organizational efficiency' cycle (day-to-day manager and staff Operational Learning) is important – but not at the expense of organizational effectiveness because one then enters, often unwittingly, the vicious spiral of 'downsize, rightsize and later capsize'. Unfortunately this is where we increasingly come face-to-face with the operational level obstacle – the MBA culture of 'analysis-paralysis' and the overdone use of financial logic and rationality at the expense of the customer's perception of and emotional attachments to a product, service or brand.

For example, it is entirely logical for banks to use the new digital technologies to reengineer their operations by cutting costs, especially in their back offices. However, applied unwisely such logic can lead to *reductio ad absurdum*. When a bank has staffed its local branch with inexperienced and cheap young staff, and created distant and ironically named 'service centres' where no-one knows you or cares about your account, it is not surprising that the rate of 'churn' of dissatisfied customers changing bank rises rapidly and wipes out the early cost gains. Similarly, when an airline 'code shares' with another airline it should not be surprised that it loses customer loyalty and their willingness to pay premium prices. The brand's image has been built personally by the customer over many years on an emotional as well as a logical basis. So when a customer telephones to make a booking they do not expect to be booked onto a flight by a different airline, with different standards of service and safety. It takes sustained Policy Learning, especially about purpose, vision and values to avoid such problems.

## Strategic Learning

So why are both examples increasingly common? What has happened to these organizations' learning and experience bases? The answer seems to be that neither customers nor their perceptions are seen as serious sources of information in the current mindsets of many of today's 'bottom-line-driven' directors and managers. So their organization's learning and experience base is squandered in pursuit of short-term gains at the expense of long-term survival and profitability. This 'organizational amnesia' does not bode well because they are creating a generation of fickle, disloyal customers who will increase the churn rate and thus increase costs dramatically. This is the exact opposite of what they set out to achieve. The organization has suffered a learning failure at all three levels of policy, strategy and operations.

Strategic Learning is about monitoring the changing external world, reviewing the organization's position in these changes, making risk assessments to protect and develop enterprise, broadly deploying its scarce resources to achieve its purpose, and ensuring that there are feedback procedures in place to measure the effectiveness of any strategy being implemented.

Learning at the strategic level must always be set in the context of agreed policies.

## THE FAILURE OF BOARDS TO COPE WITH POLICY LEARNING

Who sets these unthinking operational level priorities? Ultimate accountability lies with the board of directors. But as most directors are drawn from the operational world, and are not trained in Policy or Strategic Learning, it is hardly surprising that they neither make the time nor have the inclination to position themselves in their proper role at the strategic overlap of Operational and Policy Learning. They are rarely trained in the key directorial processes of critical review of policy and operations, risk assessment, debate, dilemma resolution and strategic decision-making processes.

If cost-reduction initiatives are generated by the top executives in lieu of policy and strategic thinking, then it takes a brave board member, or an even braver staff member, to give regular, independent critical reviews to measure the difference between what is actually happening and what was meant to happen. Bringers of bad news still tend to be shot. Yet regular, independent critical reviews are necessary at all three levels in any Learning Organization. Sadly, they rarely happen with sufficient regularity or rigour.

At the policy level of learning it is the primary role of a board to resolve the fundamental directorial dilemma of driving the organization forward while keeping it under prudent control. This is key to ensuring the customer's perception of organizational effectiveness. The constant rebalancing and learning from this fundamental directorial dilemma is the essence of the Learning Organization. It is the main task of the Learning Board. Unfortunately, at present it is seldom achieved.

I called my previous book *The Fish Rots from the Head: the Crisis in our Boardrooms* to highlight publicly my long experience that the vast majority of those executives selected to give direction to our private and public organizations are not trained to do so, nor have they much incentive to learn. Therefore, they usually avoid Policy and Strategy Learning seeing it as too difficult, challenging, time-wasting or abstract. Such executives have typically worked their way up a managerial or professional route before being given the accolade of 'director'. I use the term here as a member of the board of directors – a true 'direction-giver' – not in the US sense of someone just below the rank of vice-president. While 'board conformance' is specified increasingly and internationally through legislation and self-regulation in the field of 'corporate governance', it is much more difficult to state what constitutes good 'board performance'. It is, therefore, hardly surprising that most boards struggle on blindly doing their best. Their rate of learning is rarely sufficient, and so inevitably the fish starts rotting from the head.

The clearest statement I know of the roles of the board was spelled out in the Institute of Directors' (London) publication *Standards for the Board*. My slightly amended version sets up the four classic directorial dilemmas:

- the board must be entrepreneurial, to drive the business forward while simultaneously keeping it under prudent control;
- the board is required to be sufficiently knowledgeable about the workings of the company to be answerable for its actions, and yet to be able to stand back from the day-to-day management to retain a critical, more objective, longer-term view;
- the board must be sensitive to short-term, local issues and yet also be informed of the broader trends and competition (especially of an international nature);
- the board is expected to be focused on the commercial needs of the business while acting responsibly towards its employees, business partners, other stakeholders and society as a whole.

Three particular learning aspects stand out from this statement of directorial roles for me. First, that each role is positioned as a dynamic dilemma, not as an issue with a single resolution. This means that there is no expectation of a simple, one-off, data rational answer to any of the four dilemmas – the board's key process is to learn continuously. The art of direction-giving is to find a balance between the four classic directorial dilemmas, based on an agreed set of values and behaviours. Directors need to deploy the organization's scarce resources in turbulent environments so that they continue to achieve the organization's purpose. Seen from this perspective directing is a proper job, a continuous process, not a monthly board meeting with good food and wine as a long-term reward for having been a good manager and for promising to keep quiet in the contentious power politics of the board.

The second learning aspect is that 'directing' is a distinctly different job from 'managing'. At its simplest, managing is literally a 'hands-on' activity – the installation and maintenance of human systems to ensure control and performance from the operational, day-to-day work learning cycle. Directing is more of a 'brain-on' activity sensing and thinking about showing the way ahead, giving organizational leadership, and critically reviewing the consequences of Operational Learning. Directing requires time and money budgets to develop to competence those charged with showing the way ahead and giving leadership to their organization. How many organizations do you know that have board and director development budgets?

Third, although in the 1980s organizations were aware of many of the political and social issues surrounding organizational learning, there was little clarity or urgency about the need to ensure that directors built and maintained good relations externally with their 'stakeholders' – owners, customers, suppliers, legislators and regulators, local communities, and the physical environment – and internally with their staff. Indeed the term 'stakeholder' was not then in common use and the notion of 'worker democracy' was seen as dangerous left-wing stuff. Neither was the idea then common that many twenty-first-century organizations will rely on their staff as 'knowledge workers', and that these knowledge workers would be the key to sustained organizational learning. It was only dimly appreciated that because people are their own tools they not only have brains but also legs, and are increasingly willing to walk if the emotional climate of an organization blocks their ability to learn and develop. So rethinking and democratizing the relationships between the owners, directors, managers, and staff has become a major concern for Learning Organizations if they are to be seen as effective and efficient by their customers. A canny old factory manager put the issue to me in another way: 'for every pair of hands I hire I get a free brain! It's up to me to use it'.

Failure by the direction-givers to establish systems for developing Policy Learning by continuously sensing and learning from the changing external environment means that all other forms of organizational learning are to varying extents contaminated or disabled. How can we design and run our organizations so that all three levels of learning can operate and inform each other simultaneously to stop that rot? What are the prerequisites needed to create a Learning Organization?

# CHAPTER 2

# The Six Pre-Conditions for Creating a Learning Organization

There are six pre-conditions that need to be met by an organization before there is a hope of creating a Learning Organization.

## 1. ACCEPTING THAT ORGANIZATIONS ARE COMPLEX ADAPTIVE HUMAN SYSTEMS, NOT MINDLESS MACHINES

It is essential first to break the predominant managerial and directorial mindset that human organizations are rational, emotionless, data-logic driven machines which stay resolutely on carefully planned and predetermined tracks regardless of the changing environment, and that there is, therefore, only one correct organizational model to achieve this happy state of affairs.

It is necessary for effective directors and managers to understand and accept that their world is complex, uncertain, and has plenty of positive, and negative, emotional energies all of which affect – often in unpredictable ways – their survival. Organizations are living, or dying, organisms. I appreciate that such understanding and acceptance is against some present business school teaching. It is closer to modern physics, particularly complexity theory, with its interest in complex adaptive systems. Learning Organizations are above all complex adaptive systems and need to be understood as such. The recent interest in complexity theory should help our understanding of Learning Organizations.

Complex adaptive systems seem much closer to today's turbulent 'real world' of organizations than the recent but dated Newtonian-like idea that the world is basically a predictable, clockwork-like mechanism. David Lane of the Santa Fe Institute[9] lists amongst complexity theory's main ideas such paradoxes as:

*Chance as Cause.* Complex adaptive systems show patterns which cannot be predicted in advance, no matter how familiar the inputs. The outcomes are created by random choices, or chance, by the players. However, this does not mean that just anything can happen because constraints work as choices. In a complex adaptive system chance, rather than any immutable 'law', is the cause of the outcome. This idea alone can be highly disorientating and unnerving for many people, let alone any died-in-the-wool managerial control freak.

*Winning as Losing.* This can be restated as 'winning is not necessarily winning'. In Game theory this is what happens sooner or later when an ecology, or organization, is replaced because it has failed to respond to a new challenge. Organizations die when they cannot keep up with the rate of change in their environment. Complex adaptive systems theory describes a co-evolutionary world of many agents, or players, where 'an agent . . . that defines its success by "winning" against a currently dominant rival may find itself a victim of its own success'. Playing a new game well by the old rules does not guarantee success. Because of the chaotic instabilities introduced by multiple feedback in a turbulent world, natural selection in an obsolete, or obsolescent, context will commonly cause fitness to *decrease*, in sharp contrast to the conventional view that natural selection only and always increases fitness. This is where the inelegantly named, but very useful, concept of 'co-opetition'[10] can be brought into play to create higher order 'both . . . and' solutions to business problems – we must compete and co-operate with our competitors – rather than lower order 'either . . . or' solutions – we only compete successfully or die.

*Organizations as structures and processes.* This idea challenges scientists and managers to look at the inter-relationship of structure and process in systems to understand how they mutually determine each other. Organizations are not simply structures alone, but are energized positively or negatively by the use of appropriate human processes. These processes are people-driven and energized by their values and emotions which must, therefore, be taken fully into account.

*Rationality as limitation.* This can be summarized as 'rationality is not necessarily intelligent'. One can succeed as an organizer or director without necessarily using rational planning. Lane quotes the undoubted success of Cosimo de Medici as the head of his dynasty. He did not engage in rational planning but rather 'could feel the advantages that his structural positioning in the network offered him, and he learned how to exploit the stream of opportunities that his position kept flowing in his direction'. Note the word 'learned' here.

To many convergent-thinking, data-rational, reductionist managers and directors such paradoxes and dilemmas are highly challenging, if not downright intimidating. Yet they feel like 'the real world' to me, far away from the unreal and unthinking managerial tyranny of annual budgets, quarterly bottom-lines, and the notion that by over-focusing on increasing the efficiencies of the internal environment of our organizations we can control, or hide from, our external environment. This is patently not true and creates a picture of the rationalist manager as ostrich – head firmly buried in the operational sand exposing its backside for all the stakeholders in the policy world to kick. The ostrich will not even know where the kick came from.

## 2. UNDERSTANDING THAT ORGANIZATIONS ARE DRIVEN MORE BY PROCESS THAN STRUCTURE

Breaking the rationalist mindset to open up the diversity of organizational learning requires a process of reframing the previously accepted 'real' world. Step one is to break away from the usual mindset of an organization as a stable pyramidal structure set on solid foundations and destined to last for millennia. The average life span of a *Fortune 500* corporation is forty years and falling.

There is no single correct structure for an organization. It depends on what you are trying to achieve, the context within which you are working. And the energies of the people who comprise the organization at any given time. Classical pyramidal structures still operate as the dominant organizational model in most Latin and Confucian-influenced nations, although their effectiveness is increasingly questioned. In most other parts of the world organizational effectiveness is seen to be developing through experimentation with a combination of different structures *and* processes. These range from the inverted pyramid or 'moments of truth' structures of Jan Carlzon's Scandinavian Airlines Systems[11], through slimming down the head office function and decentralizing big organizations into a constellation of strategic business units; through creating 'federal' structures where early attempts at democratizing organizational processes by developing voting systems can be seen at ABB, the Swiss/ Swedish heavy engineering company through the rigorous development of systems thinking and multiple feedback loops across an organization, to the introduction of triple-loop learning systems as in my Learning Organization model. None of these is perfect. Yet they do suggest an historical progression towards acceptance of the power of, organizational learning and organizational democracy.

However, as the world becomes more chaotic through the growing perception of increased rates of environmental change, organizational structural change alone will not work. Structural solutions are necessary but not sufficient. Sufficiency comes only through combining structural change with human learning *processes* to develop sustainable organizational learning. These processes must turn data into usable information fast enough to allow the organization to become more responsive and sensitive to those rates of change, externally and internally, and so be able to adapt nimbly to survive. For an organization to become more sensitive means setting up systems for the continuous monitoring of its external and internal environments, checking the new information against the organization's existing purpose, vision, values, culture, strategies, and operational missions, then measuring its organizational capabilities before taking developmental or corrective actions.

As the organization, and especially the board, learns to become more sensitive to changes in the two environments it also learns to become more discriminating in its selection of appropriate information from the vast sea of data which surrounds it. Asking good, 'discriminating questions' is difficult in many organizations. So it is important for directors and managers to encourage a culture of valuing 'intelligently naive' questions[12] as a worthwhile investment of organizational resources. Most directors, managers and staff are intelligent. Yet they are also naive about many of the other functions of the business outside their own professional sphere. Encouraging intelligently naive questioning, especially in the early stages of multi-disciplinary problem-solving, can root out the many wrong assumptions, negative habits, or unquestioned working practices, which plague the effectiveness and efficiency of the organization.

Learning to ask intelligently naive, or discriminating questions, at all levels of the organization, and at all stages of the learning cycle is the key to the essential learning process of 'critical review'. If allowed to operate freely, critical review arising from such discriminating questioning reinforces learning about both organizational effectiveness and organizational efficiency. It sensitizes the organization to 'hearing the baby cry' as Colin Sworder has written[13]. When you have a baby, it is only a short time before you come to distinguish your baby's cry from all of the others. One is quickly sensitized to something, if one has the need. What is your organization's cry, and do you realize the importance of hearing it?

## 3. UNDERSTANDING THE DIFFERENCE BETWEEN FIRST AND SECOND ORDER CHANGE PROCESSES

An effective way of helping an organization to understand the nature of a Learning Organization is to generate a generally accepted model of the process of continuous organizational change. I have used the excellent work of Watzlawick, Weakland and Fisch in *Change: Principles of Problem Formation and Problem Resolution*[14] and Chris Argyris[15] on double-loop learning to build this basic model.

The work of these 'brief therapists' (on action-orientated reflective therapy) in the US and Europe has described two key aspects of individuals' and organizations' learning to understand and cope effectively with change. First, that to start an effective change process, whether modest or massive, requires some initially small modifications of both attitude and behaviour to become comfortable with the notion of change itself. These minor modifications can happen very quickly. They then allow staff to build more confidence to encourage larger scale experiments, feedback, rigorous reflection and learning, rather than relying on the collection of ever-increasing amounts of data. Over-reliance on analysis alone can kill an organization. It leads easily to 'analysis-paralysis'. Any fan of the TV series *Frasier* can watch him, or his brother, as they frequently talk themselves into inaction and frustration through a mixture of a lack of attentive listening and huge over-analysis of even the simplest problem and its likely consequences. As comedy it is very funny, but as organizational reality it is destructive. Spontaneity, energy and humanity are lost to over-analysis.

This issue has been acknowledged for a long time in organizations and has formed the basis for the long-running fight between the over-rationalist 'strategic planners' and the 'strategic thinkers'[16] in the business world. Whilst strategic planning is still rated highly in many businesses, as early as 1976 the doyen of the strategic planners, Igor Ansoff, wrote:

> Over the past twenty years it has become increasingly clear through lessons of success and failures, as well as through continuing research, that the Cartesian conception of the strategic problem suffers from two major deficiencies. First, in the language of management science, it is an "improper optimization" – the excluded variables have major impact on the preferred solution. Second, strategic planning solves only part of the total problem concerned with the maintenance of a viable and effective relationship between the organization and the environment.[17]

If too much analysis leads to inaction or sub-optimal solutions, then the way out must be action, conscious experimentation and reflective learning. Building a willingness, a commitment, to do just one simple thing that will move the issue forward, doing it successfully, and consciously learning from it, reinforces personal effectiveness in both the thought processes and the behaviours. So rather than take on an early massive commitment which may overwhelm the individual, or the organization, it is usually helpful to take small steps first and learn consciously, regularly and publicly from so doing – 'a journey of a thousand miles begins with one step'. This is the basis of 'Action Learning' to which I will return later.

This approach contrasts sharply with most people's perceptions, personal and organizational, that there is not much one can do to make changes in their organization. Many people at work feel trapped in an insensitive, uncaring and inhumane environment where inaction, avoiding risk, and hiding mistakes are preferable to experimenting, admitting mistakes and learning. 'It's more than my job's worth to make any criticisms or changes here' is the common cry. It is the cry of organizational despair. It is an indictment of the organization's lack of learning leadership and positive learning culture. If left to fester, it can create a form of organizational dis-ease which blocks its effectiveness and can turn it inwards upon itself. This is the disabling move towards creating a 'blame culture'.

In their organizations people need and strive for positive recognition of themselves as individuals and team members. Ultimately, people cannot face having no personal recognition. So if the emotional climate of the organization avoids positive recognition then, over time, rather than have no recognition at all, they will seek negative recognition. They will deliberately make mistakes, or use 'malicious obedience' – obeying orders to the letter knowing that this will either not have the outcome required by their boss, or may even have the opposite effect. But at least they will be shouted at or criticized by their executives – which is a form of recognition, and for most people definitely better than no recognition at all.

To create a more positive emotional climate, and processes for learning, it is helpful to ensure at this early stage of 'first-order change' – simple change within an existing system – that an executive faced with an issue or problem does not focus only on repeating the question 'why?'. Why? is the most powerful of all the six forms of question. Focusing on a lack of clarity over why you did something, or why something happened, is often likely to be initially disabling to a person, rather than enabling. For example, if they knew why they had made a mistake they may well not have done it. So the over-use of 'Why?' questions can lead to the highly negative emotional climate of avoiding risks and blaming others. Over-use of 'Why?' questions can turn a person towards introversion and helplessness particularly when the answer is often outside the stated dimensions of the existing problem. So the 'Why?' question needs to be used sparingly by wise directors and managers if they are to achieve effective change and a positive learning climate.

For an effective director or manager wishing to increase their people's rate of learning it is usually better to use 'How?' questions initially. These allow the exploration of the options for action, reflection and subsequent learning from that action. Using 'How?' questions for organizational learning has an energizing effect because they focus people on options, early actions, feedback and reflection for further actions which then begin to bring them out of their feeling of powerlessness. Because some people see their organizations as closed and often hostile systems they feel that if they have any options in making changes it is simply to do 'more of' or 'less of' whatever exists. This is a counsel of despair. Yet

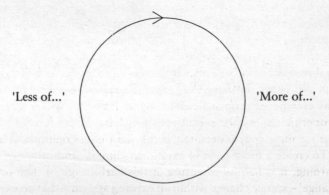

'Less of...'     'More of...'

Figure 2  First-order-change, more of . . . less of

many people spend their organizational lives in such a negative emotional state.

## Second Order Change

How does one begin to learn to move from such simplistic notions of organizational change, to reach a higher level of change? 'Second order change' requires some intellectual effort by directors and managers to cope with the more complex learning needed. One needs to develop the ability to raise one's eyes from the operational work – the immediate, the obvious, the routine and the accepted – to look further towards the horizon and so see problems and issues in a wider perspective. In executive selection terms this is known as developing a 'helicopter view'. It is used increasingly as a key indicator for the selection of high potential direction-givers. Yet it can also work just as well for any individual at any level of the organization.

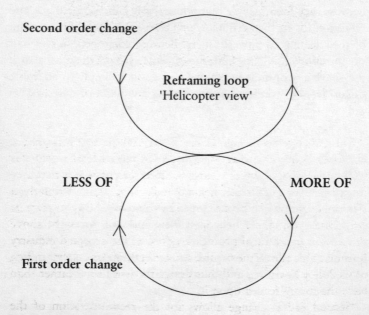

Figure 3 First and second order change processes

**Figure 4 Young woman or old woman?**

This helicopter view allows for the development of foresight, a key asset in fast-changing workplaces. In the medical world it is well-known that a sign of returning health in a patient is that they raise their eyes and literally begin to look ahead again. Similarly, a sick organization can be developed to value the ability to raise its corporate eyes, take a helicopter view and gain foresight above the current operational problems, crises, or the accepted industry formula. This allows the organization to reframe its understanding of its Policy Learning, and thus design its own future rather than have the future forced upon it.

'Second order' change allows for the reconsideration of the wider landscape, or context, of the organization. This is known

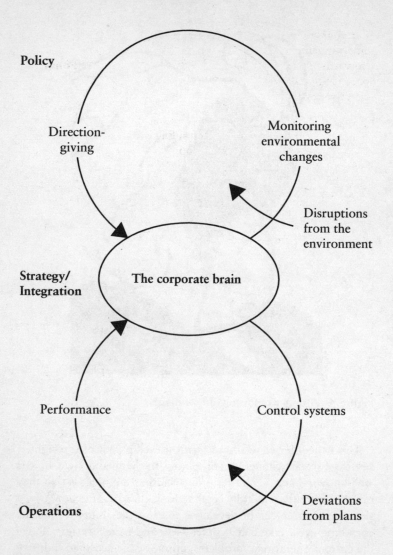

**Policy**

Direction-
giving

Monitoring
environmental
changes

Disruptions
from the
environment

**Strategy/
Integration**

The corporate brain

Performance

Control systems

**Operations**

Deviations
from plans

Figure 5(a) The double loop of learning, part 1

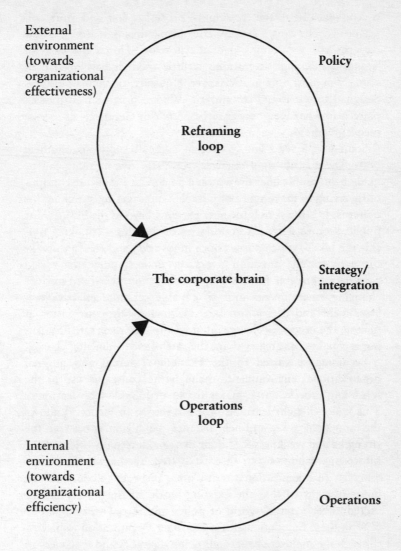

Figure 5(b)  The double loop of learning, part 2

psychologically as the 'reframing process'. You and your colleagues are drawing a better series of pictures based on the new patterns you see coming over the horizon. This is the basis of 'scenario thinking'. Reframing is little used or developed consciously in most organizations, yet. However, the human brain is designed to use it and to enjoy it. We are programmed to seek pattern in what we observe – the *gestalt* in German – as can be seen in Figure 4.

Some people see a young woman, some an old woman, others both. There is no 'right' answer, yet distinctive meaning can be made from simple lines drawn on a page. Our brains are continuously trying to make sense of complex messages by searching for patterns. It is the search for new patterns beyond the business, or public, sector's accepted boundaries of thinking – 'thinking outside the box' – which allows both innovation and creative breakthroughs for the direction-givers. By understanding the varied patterns of possible futures they become more sensitized to their changing environments and so capable of more effective risk assessment and decision-making. Ultimately they are faster at making the necessary changes that ensure that their rate of learning is equal to, or greater than, the rate of environmental change.

Becoming sensitized to the changing external and internal organizational environments through the conscious use of the reframing process is the major driver of 'double-loop learning'. This figure-of-eight learning process (shown in Figure 5) allows the individual to see and help balance the dilemmas between the strengths and weaknesses of their existing, internal world and the future opportunities and threats offered by the world outside. Similarly in organizational terms one can begin to construct the figure-of-eight so that the existing world of operations can be linked to the external world of policy and foresight.

With these foundations for a Learning Organization in place – through the mindset changes allowing directors and managers to be more comfortable with a less certain world, being sensitized to the changing environment, and being able to see opportunities and threats coming from these changes – we can move on to the next pre-condition for the design of a Learning Organization.

THE SIX PRE-CONDITIONS • 25

## 4. ACCEPTING THE NEED TO INTEGRATE THE OPERATIONAL AND POLICY/FORESIGHT LEARNING CYCLES INTO A FORUM OF STRATEGIC ORGANIZATIONAL DEBATE

In his book *Business @ The Speed of Thought*[18] Bill Gates refers frequently to the importance of the 'digital nervous system' of the organization. Remove the word 'digital' and we are back with the fundamental challenge for any group of direction-givers throughout time – how do we integrate both driving the organization forward to achieve its purpose, while keeping it under prudent control? How can we cope with not only the rates of change externally and internally but create an organizational 'central processor' which keeps our rate of learning equal to, or greater than, the rate of environmental change?

The words 'digital' and 'central processor' can give an image for many people of impersonal, technical systems buzzing away invisibly and programmed by a 'techie' with little zest for people, let alone real life. This is not my intention. I use the term 'central processor' to describe the information-gathering, values-based risk assessment and decision-taking at the heart of a Learning Organization. Legally this is the role of the board of directors. However, on their own directors are unlikely to have sufficient information, sensitivity or resources to understand simultaneously the changing external and internal environments.

A key idea of a Learning Organization is to tap continuously into the natural, daily learning of *everyone* who is a member of the organization. (At present BP Amoco is by far the most advanced corporation on this dimension[19] because of their focus on continuous learning across the organization as well hierarchically.) By so doing one can energize the Policy/Foresight, Strategy, and Operational Learning cycles. Then one can reflect on this learning by pulling these together as the focus of the organization's 'critical review and debating process' – the central processing which allows for better informed, and values-based, judgements to be made, acted upon, and learned from. This is what I label the 'corporate brain'. It is much more than just the exclusive musings of the board of directors. It is the central focus of the processes whereby the messages about the changing external and internal environments are brought together, debated seriously, risks are assessed and decisions taken affecting direction and strategy.

At the macro-political level (the world external to the organization) the understanding of changing political, economic, social, technological, and physical environmental trends is focused to increase organizational effectiveness and so become the Policy level Learning inputs into the strategic organizational debate and learning.

The inputs to this debate at the micro-political level (the internal world of the organization) are the measurements of the energies and blockages generated by the existing organizational capabilities. These should inform the strategic debate, particularly that part which will decide on the organization's ability to implement strategy effectively given the scarce resources to be deployed. Until now there has been no simple way of assessing the gap between where the organization is on each of its capabilities, and where it needs to be.

In my book *The Twelve Organizational Capabilities*[20] I suggest a way forward. I have found that Strategy Learning level, Policy and Operational Learning are integrated through critical review, strategic debate and learning processes by assessing the possibilities and risks and so giving the necessary direction. This is the Learning Organization model described in Figure 1 (p. 5). I will go into greater detail of all three learning cycles in the next chapter.

## 5. ACCEPTING AND USING THE INEVITABILITY OF 'EVENTS'

In the Learning Organization model each learning cycle has an arrow intervening and upsetting its smooth running. In the operational cycle it is the 'deviation from plans' that upsets our working lives – where we are trying to use our limited resources (via the control systems) to steer back towards plans and budgets (our performance) following unpredicted consequences from a turbulent internal world, pushing us off our plans and budgets. When the UK Prime Minister Harold Macmillan was asked what really concerned him about running an effective government he replied simply 'events'. This was the area over which he had least control.

Similarly, events disrupt the Policy Learning cycle as we try to make logical patterns from a chaotic world (monitoring the external environment), assess risks, resolve dilemmas and show the way ahead by giving leadership for the organization (direction-giving). The disruptions from the environment here can be most disconcerting to many rationalist managers and professionals as one cannot easily predict, for example, an earthquake or famine, a change of governing party, or a disruption in supplies. Indeed the 'foresight' needed here is not about having an impeccable record of *predictive* certainty of the future – in a chaotic world that is an absurd aspiration – but rather about developing systems for both being very sensitive to environmental change and having the organizational *capability* to respond quickly to events to create competitive advantage for a business or to gain scarce resources for a public sector, or not-for-profit, organization.

## 6. ACCEPTING THE PROFESSIONALIZATION OF DIRECTION-GIVERS

Here we hit a structural flaw of many organizations. Most directors have been rewarded for outstanding performance in a managerial/technical role that required very different skills from those that they need to direct their organization. They were not selected for their proven direction-giving capabilities or potential. Matters are then made worse by the fact that very few organizations have any induction, inclusion or competence-building systems in place to help their transition from the managerial/technical world to that of directorial competence. Even fewer have any regular appraisal system for assessing the competence of the direction-givers. Indeed the notion that boards of directors need regular appraisal just like anyone else is still treated with ridicule by many organizations.

The rise of the very powerful 'shareholder activist' investment funds will begin to quieten such ridicule as shareholders start to debate, assess and vote more openly and democratically on the performance of their board, and of its individual directors. Underperformance will be met increasingly by these shareholders publicly canvassing the wider shareholder base for proxy votes to change or dismiss the underperformers. This is clearly an area where the democratization of organizations is beginning to be demanded by the owners.

A consequence of the continuing selection of time-served managers and professionals as untrained directors is that the learning cycles of an organization can easily become blocked. Most training budgets and personal development plans do not reach as far as board level. So direction-givers at the centre of the 'corporate brain' are often unsure of their roles and tasks, and untrained in carrying them out. Board meetings tend then to be mechanical, legal and uncritical, with a country club atmosphere where many things are assumed rather than tested openly for fear of causing offence. Very rarely directors meet as equals taking decisions collectively under a constructive chairman. More usually critical review, independent thought, discriminating questioning and the use of 'naive intelligence' ('I don't know, but am not afraid to say so, nor to keep asking questions until I do understand') are absent in board meetings.

What happens to someone who does not use their naive intelligence – someone who knows that they are not fully competent, yet fears to ask for help because they may be seen as weak, or a wrong choice as a director? Typically after a period of some six to nine months of increasing discomfort they seek a position of comfort. They return to the roots from which they were promoted, while keeping the new car, bigger salary, stock options, the other goodies, and the title of 'director'.

This creates two major organization problems. Their unofficial return to their old managerial or professional job may feel good to them (after all, this is why they were promoted) but it creates real problems for the person now promoted to do their old job. We all feel that we can do our old job better than the new incumbent but if we then try and prove it by micro-managing their every decision we do neither party any good. If they are competent, they will resent such interference. If they are trying to reach competence rapidly, we will hinder their learning – unless we are good at coaching and can commit time to the process. My observation is that a great deal of heat and not much light is generated when a direction-giver drops down a level and tries to continue with their old functional job. Either the newcomer leaves or, more commonly, they will in turn drop down to do their old job thus setting up a knock-on effect down the organization of people being paid to do a job one or two levels above the job they actually do. This is a massive block to organizational learning.

The other consequence of such a learning block is that a vacuum is left in the direction-giving mechanism. The board is meant to be a group of equals debating on the policies, strategies and prudent control of their organization. If the majority of directors do not take up this role, and continue simply as managers, then one or two powerful people fill the vacuum and determine the way ahead, often on limited and uncriticized assumptions and data. Again, this blocks the organizational learning processes. A healthy and effective board of directors needs sufficient diversity within it to allow it to be sensitive to the changing environments and have the capacity for innovative thought and critical review.

John Argenti's list of the main causes of corporate collapse[21] is worthy of contemplation. His research suggests that there are six potential organizational problems – any three or more of which can lead to corporate collapse:

- One-man rule
- A non-participating board
- An unbalanced top team
- A lack of management depth
- A weak finance function
- A combined chairman and chief executive role

Corporate collapse may happen suddenly, but more commonly is a long, lingering death where learning systems become clogged and the emotional climate is apathetic.

One way of fighting these symptoms of corporate collapse is to first ensure that directors are aware, and committed to, the

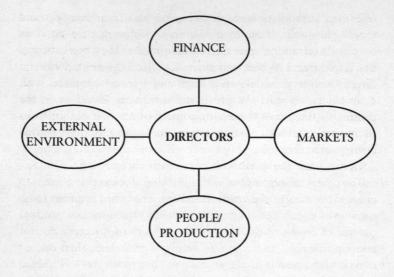

Figure 6  The traditional specialist functions

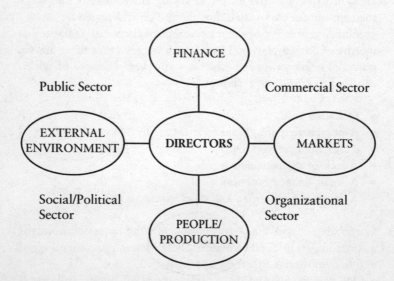

Figure 7  A transcending view of the traditional areas

four directorial dilemmas mentioned on page 9, and understand their legal duties. Then to ensure that they work through their own 'role reframing' process together so that they begin to feel the implications of the four dilemmas. John Morris's work on *Good Company*[22] shows such a reframing process. It starts with a functional view of the organization with the directors at the centre, not the top, of the organization co-ordinating the functions of finance, markets, people and production, and the external environment (Fig. 6).

Getting into the directorial reframing helicopter and climbing up to a few hundred feet, the directorial perspective begins to change by adding the contexts of the 'sectors' of commercial, organizational, social/political, and public. The functional activities of the organization now need to become sensitized to these contexts (Fig. 7).

As such sensitivity is developed it is possible to climb higher in the helicopter and begin to reframe the key elements away from

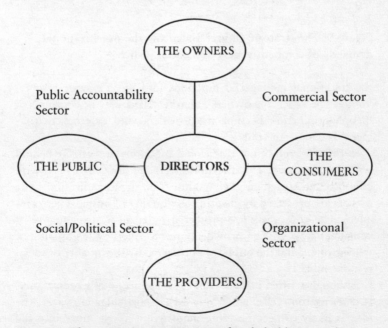

Figure 8 The strategic management of stakeholder groupings

Public Accountability
Sector

Commercial Sector

Social/Political Sector

Organizational
Sector

**Figure 9 The strategic future? Balancing the organizational demands of competitiveness and social justice**

the traditional managerial functions into more generic terms – 'finance' becomes 'the owners', 'markets' become 'the consumers', 'people/production' become 'the providers', and 'external environment' becomes 'the public'.

In the final reframing traditional functions are left far behind with the managers. The direction-givers are now challenged with creating and guarding the 'qualities' of the organization. The owners are protected by ensuring the 'quality of business performance'. The consumers are protected by ensuring the 'quality of consumer service'. The providers are protected by the 'quality of working life', and the public are protected by the 'quality of social responsibility'.

Although written in 1987 this is still conceptually radical, and is certainly not reflected in any MBA curricula. However, the idea is likely to become more mainstream as we move into the twenty-first century. The role of directing is becoming a self-regulating profession. The first sign of this is the establishment of the assessed professional qualification of 'Chartered Director' at the Institute of Directors, London.[23] Early signs are positive that existing and potential directors are willing to sign a code of conduct, undergo rigorous written examinations, submit a portfolio of directorial experience, pass an oral examination, and guarantee to undertake annual continuing professional development. Although this scheme is currently unique, I think it is likely to be the spearhead of a global movement to raise the standards of boards and individual directors.

Before this happy state of affairs arrives, if one can ensure at least that the directors are aware of, and committed to, the six pre-conditions above, then they are ready to set about creating the Learning Organization processes in detail with energy, commitment and urgency.

# CHAPTER 3

# Creating the Three Learning Cycles: Operational Learning

It is currently fashionable to be excited by the idea of 'knowledge management' (the codification and profitable dissemination of organizations' learning) and to suggest that this will be the main focus of organizations as we move into the Information Age. This idea is only partially correct. It is necessary but not sufficient. Sufficiency comes from a wider understanding of 'learning' rather than simply 'knowledge' and its management. Learning is the integration of attitudes, values and skills to complement the appropriate level of knowledge held by an individual, or an organization, to ensure its transformation into the information needed to resolve a problem. Learning is both content *and* process driven and has a moral context given by the values, attitudes and behaviours used by the individual or the organization.

A good example is seen in the developing use of the Service/Profit Chain.[24] It resolutely resists the simplistic notions that all organizations must always aim only for growth. Indeed, I keep in my head the Edward Albey aphorism that 'growth for growth's sake is the ideology of the cancer cell' as a warning against over-reliance on the concept of growth.

The basic Service/Profit Chain model stresses the crucial relationship between the retention of good customers, and the retention of competent and experienced staff and the reciprocal learning from both. I argue that 'good customers' are those that appreciate your offering as good-value-for-money, are willing to pay a small premium for your brand, are loyal and pay on time. Customers keen to value the perceived 'external quality standards' on offer are likely to be loyal. Even with the rapid growth of

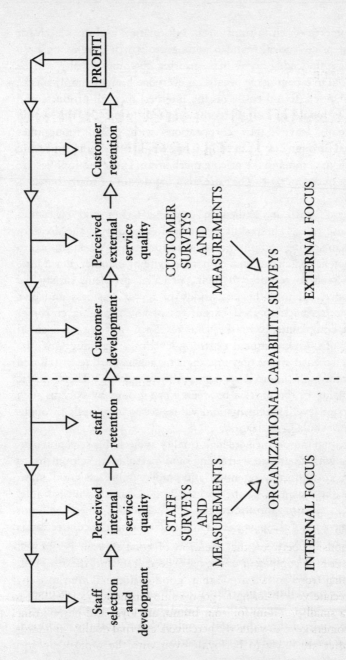

Figure 10 The Service/Profit Chain

e-commerce – rich in transparent information and the search for lowest price – loyalty and branding are worth developing by a business. Indeed, I argue that ensuring customer loyalty will be essential in e-commerce because if everyone bought simply on the lowest price (found easily on the Internet) then all products and services would quickly be commoditized. Ironically, this would eventually leave a few corporations with global monopolies created through cost leadership. They would offer little choice and be able to command the pricing mechanism. Large monopolies are highly undemocratic. They are also the dream of many business people.

'Good' staff are skilled in customer-facing and customer-response roles. These skills are found especially in the areas of problem-solving and interpersonal relationships. When trained to competence, such staff can empathize with a customer, flex a little to be seen to respond to their particular problem, satisfy the customer, enhance the probability of repeat business and give regular feedback to their executives of any changing customer needs, complaints, or market changes. Such staff are an essential driver of the Operational Learning level of a Learning Organization. To ensure that they are, their managers need to install and maintain high 'internal service quality standards'. These ensure the quality of the process between work groups by systems such as service level agreements and values-based appraisals throughout the whole organization.

Of equal importance are high-quality and reliable selection processes with guaranteed training and personal development to ensure cost-effective retention and employability of 'good' staff. All of these aspects of the Service/Profit Chain are measurable. Sadly in most organizations few are. Such measurements will not become part of the new executive mindset until the connection is made by all parties of the *learning* link between retaining and growing good customers, and retaining and growing good, problem-solving staff.

While the ability to turn data into information to solve problems is a key 'hard' organizational capability, the personal capacity and attitude of the individual problem-solver, and the emotional climate for learning in the organization – the key 'soft' capabilities

– also need to be valued before determining an organization's competence. This is rarely understood by boards and managers and so tends to be derided as sociological claptrap. Yet organizations are as much driven by emotions as rationality. When I point out that all such 'hard' and 'soft' capabilities are measurable there is often a deafening silence. This is news to a great many people but they soon get the hang of it and then find the regular measuring of key organizational capabilities essential for the control of their organization. The details of such measures are revealed in greater depth in my book *The Twelve Organizational Capabilities*[25].

It stresses that we can, and must, measure learning at all three levels of a Learning Organization – triple-loop learning. Indeed, I argue that it is essential for all three levels of learning to be measured regularly and rigorously if you are to create and sustain a Learning Organization. How do you start doing that?

## OPERATIONAL LEARNING

Operational Learning is the day-to-day learning which we all do all of the time. We may learn wittingly or unwittingly – good or bad things – but we learn all the time. The big problem is that most of us do it unconsciously, habitually, and with little sense that it should be valued or communicated in any way to anyone else. We may be individually good at Operational Learning but without organizational processes which give the consequent learning regularity and rigour it is difficult to be aware of it, or to use it effectively.

At its simplest level Operational Learning is the continuous process of moving people towards conscious competence within their organization. If one creates a traditional quadrant with 'competence' and 'consciousness' as the two axes (Figure 11) then one has four possible combinations:

Unconscious Incompetence   where people do not know that they do not have the necessary attitudes, knowledge and skills to be competent

| Unconscious Competence | where people do a good job but without consciousness of this or of the need to communicate their learning to others |
| Conscious Incompetence | where people are aware of their lack of attitudes, knowledge and skills but choose to do nothing about them |
| Conscious Competence | where people do a good job and are able to share their learning with others – the aspiration of any learning individual or Learning Organization |

In the day-to-day world of operations the seeking of conscious competence as a key aim of a Learning Organization relies on the relationship between a person and their manager or supervisor. For this relationship to be positive sustainably, both the rational (work-orientated) and emotional (personal process-orientated) aspects of work must be consciously addressed by both parties. To do this effectively two aspects of the line manager's role need to be clarified and codified for all to understand.

First, that there is a recognized sequential development process for all staff. This is the responsibility of the line manager, whether for a junior supervisor or the chairman of the board. The capability of developing staff to competence is an important and assessable aspect of the line manager's role and must be built into his or her job description and appraisal process.

The basic process of personal development is well-documented[26] and progresses over time to levels of maturity in a job:

| Induction | the introductory process by which people get to know the technical aspects of their work, the health and safety requirements, and all those 'hard' aspects which are the building blocks of competence. This is usually handled well by line managers until one reaches the executive and directorial levels of an organization when, mysteriously, it disappears completely. |

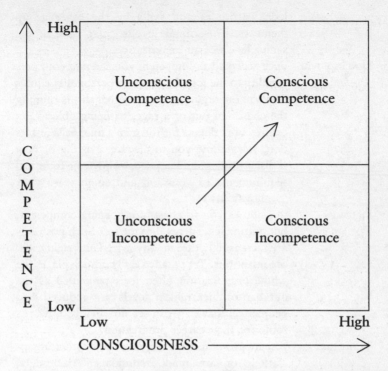

Figure 11 Towards conscious and competent learning

Inclusion    this is a key developmental process which most
             line managers miss out. It is the simple, five-
             minutes-a-day coaching to ensure that the new
             member is accepted socially as a useful new team
             member. It is not hearts-on-sleeve stuff – just the
             basic protection, and development, of your invest-
             ment in your new human asset.

Competence   you need induction *and* inclusion to be able to
             demonstrate your competence within your new
             group. No matter how technically capable you
             are, you cannot realize your full potential unless
             accepted, included and allowed to use your know-

Development once accepted as competent you can add your personality to the job. A job plus a personality equals a role in the organization. Whether this is calming the chairman out of a rage, or being able to get centre court tickets for the men's final at Wimbledon, roles allow you to develop existing or new skills, attitudes and knowledge above the technical requirements of your job and so increase your 'employability'.

Plateau this allows you to coast along, being competent, but putting less energy into the job. Such positions are increasingly rare in 'downsized and rightsized' organizations. Yet paradoxically in such places the whole organization often feels plateaued as the number of hierarchical levels are reduced and people feel that they can see no obvious upwards route for their career progression.

Transition you are promoted, retired, move to another organization, or are made redundant. Alarmingly, twenty-five per cent of UK executives die before their sixty-fifth birthday, which is the big transition. The actuaries bank on this, and this percentage is considered quite good by world standards.

If a line manager's job specification is clearly to take each staff member through this developmental cycle, and to assess each stage of it – and for the line managers to be assessed in turn – then a firm foundation, and a constructive emotional climate, for Operational Learning will be established.

The building blocks needed above this foundation, start with another specific task in the line manager's job description. At the beginning or end of each day (or piece of work), it is crucial that the line manager asks, gets answers to, and records four simple questions:

ledge, attitudes and skills by the other group members. This can be a particular issue at the senior levels of an organization.

- what went right? This should be celebrated with a genuine 'thanks' each time. Managers not saying 'thanks' for a job well done are one of the biggest obstacles to learning in all cultures that I come across.
- what went wrong? Whether the problem requires instant action or later reflection, this must be recorded and studied so that emerging patterns of mistakes can be seen, publicized and learned from by others.
- what can be done about this? Encourage problem-solving, action-learning processes and commitment at the lowest levels possible in the organization to build sustainable operational learning capability.
- who else needs to know? Organizations are complex and unpredictable, so decisions and actions taken in one place will certainly affect others, even if the consequences are unknowable. Again, ensuring continuous dialogue and critical review between all parts of the organization – horizontally as well as vertically – and ensuring that reliable performance measures and problem pattern identification systems are in place to anchor that debate, are fundamental to developing a learning climate.

With the personal development process and the line manager's regular 'critical review' and questioning systems in place, one can then begin to raise one's sights, to take a 'helicopter view' of the level of Operational Learning.

Figure 12 reviews what happens when a mistake is made, or when there is a deviation from our operational plans. It makes some heroic assumptions, especially that it is possible to ensure that all people will accept responsibility for a mistake or deviation quickly and openly. However, such an emotionally intelligent 'learning climate' can be developed. Indeed it is necessary to do so if one wishes to avoid creating a blame culture with its corrosive consequences. A positive learning climate can be seen in the UK in such companies as Jaguar, Rover, BP Amoco and Unipart. At Jaguar the circular production line is designed to be largely self-managed. So if a car completes its cycle and is not perfect then the staff themselves have the power to discipline the offending

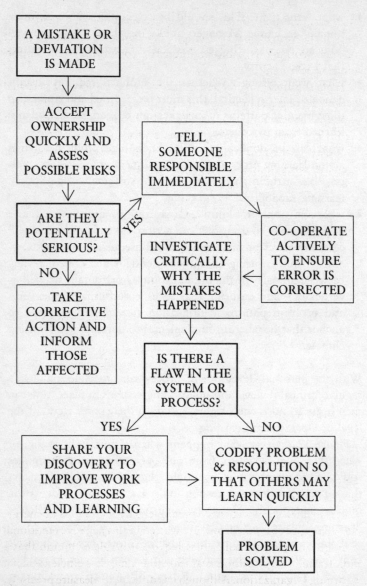

**Figure 12 The Learning Organization: the idealized process of critical review and learning (adapted from Keith Grint, Templeton College, Oxford)**

workers. Learning climates can be developed and sustained – but only if the vast majority of employees can see the positive effect on their working lives and are therefore committed to the importance of learning.

From this fundamental acceptance of responsibility for personal actions there is a simple flow of decisions as to the relative importance of the learning opportunity and who else must be informed about it so that others may be aware of it in future.

Whatever the priority, the essence is to develop the rigour and regularity of systematic Operational Learning by:

- co-operating actively to first resolve the issue
- then codifying the problem, so that the 'corporate memory' is not lost
- then reflecting on the wider organizational issues to determine the pattern of problems emerging
- then informing the wider organization of the pattern, and of the corrective actions taken
- and finally asking for feedback on the consequences of your actions and learning on the rest of the organization

This is not an easy ride. It challenges and later expands many people's view of their responsibilities and accountabilities in an organization.

However, it is a more comfortable and profitable process than the reverse – the non-learning organization. At the level of Operational Learning this is full of blockages and has an emotional climate that encourages hiding mistakes and blaming others until the organization goes into a vicious and energy-destroying cycle of recrimination.

It is plain to see in Figure 13 that much larger amounts of energy, and therefore cost and profit, are wasted in this negative emotional climate. Some of my colleagues reckon as a rule of thumb that a non-learning organization is at least four times less efficient than a Learning Organization. Although it is difficult to measure precisely, this factor is certainly worth considering seriously. Most of the organizations I have seen or worked with have been, or have large sections which are, non-learning organizations.

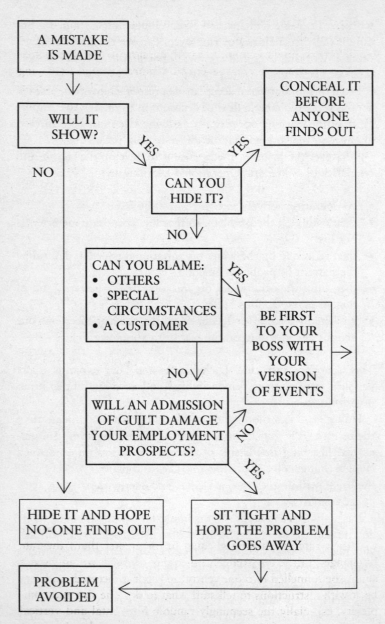

Figure 13 The 'non-learning' organization

In truth it is not that they are not learning at all. They are just learning all the wrong things – how to hide mistakes, how to blame others, how to commit to nothing, how to avoid responsibility, and how to exert least energy to retain their soul-destroying jobs. They are, like the Bourbon kings, doomed to 'learn nothing and forget nothing'. It is their directors and managers that create the negative emotional climate and organizational systems which encourage organizations either not to learn consciously, or to forget too quickly. Such 'organizational amnesia' has a debilitating long-term effect and leads ultimately to corporate collapse or take-over. Over time it creates an organizational culture – the webs of signification we have spun for ourselves and by which we are then constrained – which is essentially negative and inhumane. What can be done to counter this at the operational, day-to-day level of learning?

## The democratization of organizations through learning

Two approaches are evolving which show the slowly growing democratization processes of organizations through developing systems of organizational learning that involve all members of the organization:

- the devolution of the power to learn consciously and openly at work
- the development of more integrated thinking about organizational structures and processes

### DEVOLUTION OF THE POWER TO LEARN CONSCIOUSLY AND OPENLY AT WORK

If we are to create organizations that have the ability to ensure that their rate of learning is equal to (or greater than) the rate of change in their environment, then day-to-day learning cannot simply be funnelled into one centralized spot, processed, and sent back with instructions to tell staff what to do. The size and complexity, especially the seemingly random horizontal and vertical communications of organizations, do not allow for this. Learning is as widely distributed as there are members of the organization. Everyone learns all the time at work. The problem is that we do not usually have the systems for capturing and critically reviewing that learning, nor the emotional climate for encouraging people to be open about their learning, and to be willing to share it. Operational Learning tends to be personal, secretive and essentially negative – we learn what not to do so that we can survive despite the organization. How can one reverse such a negative learning process and climate among the staff?

A useful method is for the directors and executives to accept that they have only a limited control of the rate, and the content, of the Operational Learning of their staff. They need to accept and act upon the idea that the organization's effectiveness and efficiency are not defined in the customer's mind by the quality and magnificence of the directorial and executive thought, but rather by the customer's daily experiences with 'customer-facing' staff. These employees are rarely senior in the organization. They are more likely to be the salesperson, check-in clerk, telephone operator, delivery driver or maintenance person. Encouraging them to take up their power, right and duty to learn at work is a democratizing process.

There are some powerful organizational structures and processes which demonstrate this. Perhaps best known is Jan Carlzon's inverted pyramid or 'moments of truth' organizational structure[27]. Whereas most people see their organization as a pyramidal hierarchy in which all the positions are fixed, and where they have little or no power of discretionary action, Jan Carlzon reversed this mindset in his organization. On taking over the ailing Scandinavian Airlines System (SAS) in the late 1970s he realized that the only people who could ensure the survival of the organization were the customers – and they were disenchanted. The source of their disenchantment was the attitude and low quality of service of the staff when dealing with their customers. The meeting between a staff member and the customer he defined as 'the moment of truth' for SAS. It was reckoned then that they had some five million moments of truth each day, that around eighty per cent were unsatisfactory, and that a disgruntled customer told an average of six other people about their bad experience. So at its worst SAS was causing some twenty four million bad messages a day to be transmitted about itself. How many moments of truth a day does your organization have; how many of those are bad; how do you know about these; and do you have systems for learning continuously from this data?

Jan Carlzon's approach was to get everyone in the organization to change their mindset about organizing so that they understood and agreed to invert the pyramid, to put the customer on top – after all this is where you get paid – were well-serviced by the customer-facing staff, backed by a rejuvenated level of first-line managers. He then gave these two customer-facing levels two key resources. First, small amounts of discretionary power to allow some flexability to meet individual customer needs. Second, some very basic training in problem-solving and interpersonal skills so that staff could identify and respond to those customer needs.

## DELEGATION AND DEMOCRATISATION

As the old mindset of organizations as permanent, pyramidal structures driven by a single omniscient leader disappears, the chances for fragmentation and confusion rise sharply. Who will now have power; and what sort of power? Without an agreed single leader won't we spend our time fighting for power and so lose sight of the purpose of the organization? Will our staff be capable of accepting delegated power? These are legitimate questions. It is wise to air such doubts. Yet the evidence is already there that the thoughtful delegation of power to the lowest level possible in an organization is a highly beneficial, energising and democratising process. Staff greatly appreciate their personal recognition as responsible people, willing to learn for the good of the whole, if discretionary power is delegated to them.

The privatisation of British Airways in 1987 resulted in a remarkably fast transformation in the public's perception of BA's service. From a classically customer-unfriendly, surly state-owned company it took just three years for noticeable changes to occur. By using the Carlzon 'moments of truth' ideas, inverting the operational pyramid so that the customer was acknowledged by all to be on top, and that the customer-facing staff are the publicly perceived, leading edge of the business, BA set about transforming mindsets and values inside and outside its business. This was not done in a top-down-first project but rather by the mass application of simple training followed by the encouragement and reward of effective behaviours on the job.

The start of the transformation process was the *Putting the Customer First* training programme. This was linked to the firm statement by the chief executive that without satisfied repeat customers no-one would have a job in BA. Every staff member worldwide in the customer-facing category went through this two-and-a-half-day programme. It was focused on markedly improving the handling of customers to ensure their satisfaction with BA service and so increase the likelihood of their repeat business. Basic problem-solving and interpersonal skills training was given to over ten thousand staff in some three years. Then when a customer had a problem rather than give a short yes or no answer – based on a strict set of rules behind which the staff member could hide – they were encouraged to listen attentively to both the content and the emotional tone of the question and to respond as empathetically as possible (using a little personal discretion where necessary) to either resolve or at worst ease the problem.

This approach was very effective and BA's passenger numbers and profits soared. Although an individual staff member's or their supervisor's levels of discretionary decision-taking were not high, the effect on staff was positive and long-lasting. They were recognized increasingly by their bosses as intelligent and vital people within the system. The supervisors saw their proper role reinstated after years of erosion and, very importantly, every staff member on the training programme met the then Chief Executive, Sir Colin Marshall, face-to-face to discuss issues. He encouraged them to return to their base, learn from their work and feed this learning back into subsequent *Putting the Customer First* programmes. This energized BA for many years as the idea of learning continuously at work was seen to pay off handsomely for all concerned – staff, bosses and customers.

However, the consequences of delegating some discretionary power to the customer-facing staff and supervisors, forced reconsideration of the middle manager's roles and tasks. This was not such an easy and obvious process to handle. The managers installed and maintained the organizational systems and monitored the day-to-day results. Although the delegation process allowed them more time for these key aspects of their jobs many managers felt frustrated that they were not now expected to intervene on all aspects of real-time problems. The micro-management of 'their' patch had been removed by the new powers granted to the customer-facing staff through the *Putting the Customer First* programmes. So the managers, too, needed retraining around a new value-set and new learning and reward criteria, particularly concerning the issue of creating continuous customer satisfaction through better people management.

The consequence was the *Managing People First* programme. This was rolled out over three years. It had an impact, but it was not as emotionally powerful as that generated by the customer-facing staff programme. The results for the managers were not so clear-cut nor easy to see quickly. Combined with many managers feeling a loss of power, and uncomfortable with their new role, they proved slower to make significant change personally or organizationally. This is not to suggest that no change happened, it did and it made a positive contribution, but the process was longer and slower than predicted. From Nick Georgiades' public statement, that they could change the culture of BA in a year, I would argue that at the managerial level it was at least three years before noticeable changes flowed. The lack of rapid feedback as the systems were changed often inhibited the managers' learning processes.

In 1997, some ten years after launching massive retraining programmes, BA relaunched its training schemes following a tail-off in financial performance after many years of above average returns. This time the focus is on improving the customer's experience in the front-end of the aeroplane – business and first class. It will be interesting to see if BA can recapture the initial emotional drive of the *Putting the Customer First* initiative or whether the recent years of apparently fixating on the bottom-line performance have stifled the willingness of staff to learn regularly and rigorously from their work.

Encouraging staff to learn openly and share that learning is increasingly seen as the key to organizational survival and development – public, private or not-for-profit – in the twenty-first century. Sir John Browne, Chief Executive Officer of BP Amoco, encourages his large yet increasingly adaptive company to accept organizational learning as central to their work. In a definitive *Harvard Business Review* interview[28] entitled *Unleashing The Power Of Learning* he makes the point that 'learning is at the heart of a company's ability to adapt to a rapidly changing environment'. BP Amoco has developed the notion of the 'Virtual Team Network' – 'a computer network designed to allow people to work co-operatively through sharing knowledge quickly and easily regardless of time, distance and organizational boundaries'. This PC-based system allows e-mail, video-conferencing, electronic blackboards, scanners, faxes and groupware, plus an intranet with a massive number of home pages. Everyone in BP has the capability and authority to create his or her own home page.

The $12 million pilot scheme was launched in BP Exploration in 1995. Amongst the results Browne lists are:

- a big drop in the work hours needed to solve problems as a result of improved interactions between land-based drilling engineers and off-shore rig crews
- a significant decrease in the number, and cost, of helicopter trips to off-shore oil platforms
- the avoidance of a refinery shutdown because technical experts at another location were able to examine a corrosion problem remotely
- a reduction in reworking during construction projects because designers, fabricators, construction workers, and operations people could collaborate more effectively.

BP estimates that the 'virtual team network' alone produced at least $30 million in value in its first year.

Sir John Browne is going further. He says that 'the wonderful thing about knowledge is that it is inexpensive to replicate, if you can capture it'. He wants to extend such organizational knowledge by developing his IT/knowledge management systems to aid the development of 'learning communities'. Each of the forty business units in BP Exploration is a member of one of four peer groups faced with common problems from which they are expected to learn while sharing technical information. There is no boss in these learning communities because Browne says:

> if you had a boss, you would have an organization and a hierarchy, or hierarchies, or, more specifically, the politics that accompany hierarchies. And which hamper the free exchange of knowledge. People are more open with their peers: they are more willing to share and to listen, and much less likely to take umbrage when someone disagrees with them. Regardless of the team, if it is not operating on a peer basis, it is not going to get the right interactions. It might sound like fantasy but I firmly consider myself only the first among equals in the top management team.

Here is a chief executive giving positive reinforcement to the practice of continuous learning, especially horizontally across the organization. His approach is the opposite of generating the 'blame culture' and relying on the old vertical hierarchy to sort out problems. It is underpinned by the use of information management systems that reinforce the drive for more informed, democratic choices in organizations. Whether it is a personal home page, a bulletin board, the introduction of learning communities, or increasing the levels of staff members' decision-making powers, we are seeing an apparently quiet unstoppable move towards more organizational accountability, probity and transparency in private and public organizations. This is organizational democracy in action.

## ACTION LEARNING – THE ENGINE OF THE LEARNING ORGANIZATION AND ORGANIZATIONAL DEMOCRACY

The growing use of conscious learning systems at work by such companies as BA, BP Amoco, Conoco, Unipart, Jaguar and BMW Rover causes me to revisit the long-known but under-appreciated process of 'action learning'. I see that the ability of individuals and groups to learn consciously, regularly and rigorously from their work is the core competence of a Learning Organization.

The essential philosophy and technology of action learning was developed in the period 1947–50 by Professor Reg Revans at the newly-nationalized UK National Coal Board. Revans' stature as a remarkable mathematician and statistician was established at Cambridge before he became a member of the Coal Board's Intelligence Unit. Here, under Sir Geoffrey Vickers, he worked with such distinguished colleagues as Fritz Schumacher and Jacob Bronowski. Their later individual published output included *Small is Beautiful*, *The Ascent of Man*, *Freedom in a Rocking Boat* and *Science and the Manager*. Revans applied his mathematical skills at the operational level to statistical studies of the relationship between size and safety in the coal mines. This work led him underground to study the human aspects of his statistics – which showed a significant rise in accidents once the size of a pit rose above one thousand men. Acceptance underground of an ex-Cambridge don was not easy for gritty Yorkshire and Scots miners. His early, lonely existence was changed unexpectedly by a hidden competence. At Cambridge he had been in the UK Olympic shot-putt team for the 1932 Los Angeles Olympics. One of the miners' underground relaxations was putting bets on who amongst their mates could throw a rail fish-plate the furthest. Once Revans demonstrated his skill by beating his own team, he became their secret weapon – winning them some serious bets and thus becoming accepted as a full member of the team. Miners do not expect dons to be able to throw fish-plates any distance at all so the odds for the home team were always good.

His inclusion allowed him to study in great detail the learning processes which occurred naturally within, and between, groups of men whose very existence underground depended on learning continuously to guarantee their individual and corporate safety. Over time he was able to derive a theory of 'learning circles' where the regular and rigorous reflection on current learning, and the careful design and piloting of safety improvements, led to a drastic reduction in the number of accidents. These learning circles were, incidentally, one of the few ideas picked up by the Japanese Productivity Council's tour of the US and Europe in 1950. They were searching for ways of improving post-war Japanese productivity and quality standards building on the immediate post-war work of Deming and Juran. The Japanese took the notion of learning circles and developed them as 'quality circles'.

Through his work Revans highlighted the difference between 'clever managers' (technical specialists and experts with convergent thinking styles) and 'wise managers' (those with divergent thinking styles who see the wider picture by asking discriminating, intelligently naive, questions of the experts). He argues that 'we have lots of clever people around our organizations who can answer our technical puzzles, but we have very few people who can isolate the organizational problem by asking the right question in the first place'. He argues that much time and money is spent in organizations (in my terms) generating schools of 'campus-thinkers'. In these people get their job satisfaction by being seen to be clever against each other, putting down the ideas of others and pushing through often ill-considered plans, rather than rising above the micro-politics of the organization to take wise direction-giving decisions. In most organizations there comes a point where such a negative organizational climate kills its ability to learn and allows what has learned to be forgotten. This is where 'organizational amnesia' appears.

Revans argues that most specialized, 'clever', learning is of highly codified information which he calls 'programmed' or 'P' Learning. Formal education systems are designed to provide only this type of learning. He argues that what is needed by direction-givers, and useful members of any society, is the ability to ask discriminating questions – which he calls 'Q' Learning – of the pre-programmed learning so that the specialist inputs can be optimized while the strategic perspective is kept. This holistic approach to learning is central to action learning. Direction-givers need to learn the art of discriminating questioning so that they are not swamped by the 'techno-babble' of the experts. Revans says that effective direction-givers 'look after their Ps and Qs' using the formula:

Learning = Programmed Knowledge +

Discriminating Questioning

$$L = P + Q.$$

I have found that the majority of direction-givers in an organization find this formula helpful in learning how to stop themselves being dragged into the mire of micro-managing their organization. People from a single specialist background can be a little unsettled by it at the start of a personal development process, but once grasped it increases their effectiveness dramatically.

In *The ABC of Action Learning*[29] Revans describes his view of the four major blockages to such personal development – 'the four corrigible handicaps':

- the idealization of past experience
- the charismatic influence of other successful managers
- the impulse to instant activity (rather than thought)
- the belittlement of subordinates

One can picture the type of director or manager who craves action rather than thought and believes that the way in which things were done before is of key importance. One has met them many times before. They play down the importance of having the imagination, the moral courage, and the confidence to think seriously about how things must be done in future. Such people are infected by the 'not invented here' syndrome, are over-concerned about 'how old so-and-so would have done it', are focused on habit and gut reactions, rather than reflective thought, and fail to use or encourage the learning of their subordinates.

This exposes their organization to unnecessary risk. In any organization there is an ever-present element of risk and as the rate of external change rises, so does the need for informed risk-taking. Developing higher quality questioning is essential to creating authentic information, and so to learning and reducing risk. The application of technical knowledge alone is not sufficient to resolve complex organizational problems. Even if it were, the intervention

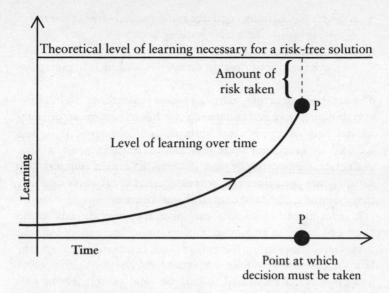

Figure 14  Managerial risk-taking – an assessment of typical risk taking during problem solving

of time as a variable ensures managers rarely have enough information to take a risk-free decision. It is axiomatic that executive decisions are usually taken before there is time to get the full facts. The difference between the level of learning held by the executive and the theoretical total needed for a risk-free decision is a measure of the amount of risk taken.

## Making Action Learning Work for a Learning Organization

People learn naturally at work. However, not all that they learn is positive from the organization's viewpoint. To encourage positive, constructively critical learning four elements need to be designed into the action learning process to ensure a cost-effective return:

- a crucial organization issue is identified and then used as a learning project
- authority is given to the action learning group to take thoughtful action on this issue

- a system for learning regularly and rigorously from the project is established in the action learning group
- participants volunteer who are willing to take thoughtful risks on the issue and so develop themselves and their organization

The design of an action learning process is simplicity itself. However, building trust and competence for this to become an organizational way of life is more difficult and long-term. It is best handled by launching some pilot action learning projects first, evaluating them carefully and publicly, and then building this learning into the values and behaviours that are rewarded so that they become part of the organizational culture.

It helps greatly if a senior executive, reporting directly to the chief executive, is appointed as director of the action learning programme. Appointing this person is not necessarily the responsibility of Human Resources. Line managers are just as competent and often better motivated to find the right person for the job. The role is demanding and micro-political – good training for a general managership or directorship. Programme managers learn quickly that there is not necessarily a direct relationship between the logic of an action and its acceptance by those involved in its implementation – they learn to balance the task-orientated needs of the top team with the willingness of staff to carry them out.

Having gained the top team's willingness to delegate authority

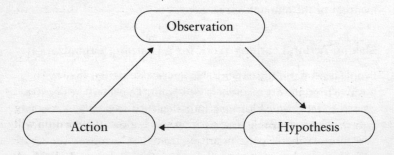

**Figure 15 The action-fixated learning cycle**

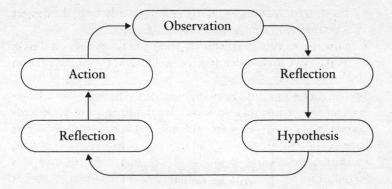

**Figure 16 The action Learning cycle**

to change, and the commitment of the action learning group to proceed, the next stage is one of the design of the action learning groups. Action learning groups need a structure which links analysis, reflection, prognosis, implementation, reflection and testing in a systematic way. Members of the group should be 'colleagues in adversity' – who will respect the confidentiality of the personal experimentation and learning of each group member. They are expected to give (and receive) constructive criticism, personal support and honest feedback within the group. They create the rigour and pace of the action learning, throughout the organization, through the regularity of their meetings. From this reflective process organizations can break away from the action-fixated cycle of non-learning which so bedevils many of our companies and corporations.

The action-fixated learning cycle is shown in Figure 15 and is contrasted with the action learning cycle shown in Figure 16.

When projects are integrated into an organization-wide, action learning-base transformation process, then not only is learning continuously available from each project but the organization will see more easily the patterns arising from that learning – see Figure 17. This is the great pay-off from action learning. Individual, group, project, and organizational learning are focused on at the same time.

Successful action learning programmes seem to have specific

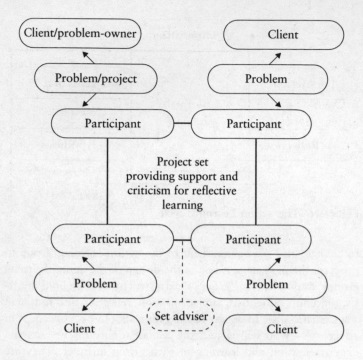

**Figure 17 The integration of live projects into an action learning programme**

characteristics which depend on a combination of project types. The matrix is described in Figure 18.

This shows the range, although full-time or part-time projects can be added to create a third dimension to this figure. Experience shows that:

- 'own job' projects are effective for personal development, especially as part of the induction, inclusion and competence phases at the start of a job;
- 'internal exchanges' (exchange projects within the organization) tend to be effective for personal development, and for establishing more effective horizontal organizational links between specialist functions within the organization, or with suppliers;
- 'external exchanges' (exchange projects between organizations)

|  | Own job | Other job |
|---|---|---|
| Own organization | Own job projects | Internal exchange projects |
| Other organization | Technical expertise exchanges | External exchanges |

**Figure 18 Types of action learning projects**

tend to be highly effective for personal development, and for the organization to widen its perspective, and value the diversity of the changing world in terms of understanding better customer needs and the wider socio-political environment;

- 'technical exchanges' (can be either internal or external exchanges) tend to have limited usefulness for action learning group purposes or the development of organizational problem-solving capacity. They tend to over-concentrate on the solution of technical puzzles, and generate destructive 'not invented here' battles. With very careful handling they can be used for the horizontal transfer of best practice.

In recent years the fixation by senior executives on the bottom-line has led to the rise of many team-based action learning programmes. These can be effective at quickly resolving organizational problems, but can encourage the non-learning 'quick fix' mentality and so often undervalue the importance of personal truly effective action learning programmes and the consequent rise of a conscious 'action learning culture' in the organization.

Fundamental to this culture is the idea that for any organizational change to occur there has to be a simultaneous convergence of three types of organizational power. Revans characterizes this 'coalition of powers' as:

- Who Knows? (Information power)
- Who Cares? (Emotional energy power)
- Who Can? (Formal power)

Although such a coalition may never meet face-to-face, it is the action learning group's role to ensure that these powers are aligned so that change can happen effectively. Developing a coalition-building competence is a key aspect of both personal and organizational action learning.

The process is powerful. In 1996 Unipart saved some £300,000 in accident reduction through such an action learning process. United Biscuits cut its accident insurance premiums by 20 per cent in two years and saw a drop of 60 per cent in liability claims against a national rise of 17.5 per cent.

The identification of key issues blocking organizational progress – whether in Operational, Strategy or Policy Learning – is the basis for launching an action learning programme. Delegating power to small, diverse, committed learning groups to learn consciously and regularly in real-time and to implement their solutions by energizing the rest of the organization creates the engine for change in the organization. Taken over time it creates the learning climate, and ultimately the culture, of that organization. Action learning is the engine of change, and of the gradual democratization of organizations through the development of better sharing of learning, leading to more informed choices at all levels of an organization.

## Twelve Organizational Capabilities

How can one define and measure the key organizational issues on which to build an action learning programme? My wife Sally and I have developed a simple measure for this which was published recently in *The Twelve Organizational Capabilities*. Within the twelve dimensions of:

- Adaptiveness
- Work Quality
- Clarity of Personal Responsibility
- Financial Rewards
- Personal Rewards
- Organizational Clarity
- Personal Performance Indicators
- Group Performance Indicators
- Learning Climate
- Leadership
- Customer Orientation
- Competitor Orientation

we have found sufficiency to cover all organizational issues in the many corporate and national cultures with which we have worked. Each dimension is measurable to find the difference between where a respondent sees their organization now, and where they think that it needs to be to achieve its objectives. These differential measures can be asked also of customers, suppliers, and even competitors in some circumstances, to maximize the information as to where you need put your scarce resources to be as effective and efficient as possible. From these measures the direction-givers can see on one or two sheets of paper the statistical analysis of organizational issues, especially blockages. They can then launch carefully focused action learning groups to rapidly resolve their current organizational issues while simultaneously creating a long-term culture of organizational learning.

## OPERATIONAL LEARNING VALUES: ACCOUNTABILITY, PROBITY AND TRANSPARENCY

As software advances and the law begins to demand more regular, more transparent and much higher quality feedback on the risk assessment and internal control mechanisms of an organization –

the legal duty to keep its operations under 'prudent control' – we begin to see the emergence of another aspect of organizational learning which directly influences democracy at work. Although we do not have an organizational Freedom of Information Act yet, trends are beginning to set the ground for such legislation. The promulgation of a law for the protection of 'whistleblowers' is a good example. In business it is likely that such developments will come through tougher rules on the disclosure of accurate performance figures, and risk assessment processes, to shareholders and staff as well as at least some stakeholders.

Two forces are driving this trend in business. On the one hand are the growing number of 'shareholder activists', particularly pension fund owners and managers, who want to ensure that the direction-givers to whom they have delegated their 'duty of trust' hold the organization in safe hands for future generations.

On the other hand is the growing national and international pressure for better systems of monitoring operational performance and ensuring higher quality risk assessment. A growing number of countries have sufficient political concerns over the competence of their direction-givers to want to ensure proper compliance, or 'conformance', in future. Two processes seem to be happening simultaneously. First, initiatives are under way in some countries to codify the necessary procedures, processes, values and behaviours needed to measure operational performance. For example, in the UK the recent discussion paper of the *Turnbull Report* (1999)[30] shows a way ahead by suggesting more rigorous codification of the risk analysis process for each organization, and the declaration of the consequences at least annually to the owners. This has been well-received and is likely to become accepted throughout the Commonwealth over time, thereby affecting over a quarter of the world's population.

Second, new software is appearing which not only displays operational performance information by moving trendlines, rather than purely numbers, but has the added attraction of having 'intelligent agents' built into the system to help ask discriminating questions so that the implications of the inter-relationships of the figures are fully appreciated. The best example I know of this new software is being developed by Streamline in Sydney.[31]

As operational performance systems come on-line it is easier for directors, shareholders and legislators to check that the fundamental values of corporate governance – accountability, probity and transparency – are being upheld and learned from by the directors and managers. As more and more global agencies such as the World Bank, the Commonwealth Association for Corporate Governance, the International Monetary Fund, and the Organization for Economic Co-operation and Development begin to insist on the importance of these values, and the adoption of them by organizations, learning from them will become essential for business success.

## The End of the Tyranny of Twelve-Month Budgets

The development of such values, and their back-up software, suggests to me that we already have more transparency in organizational decision-making and so will be more able to easily see the *pattern* of future operational performance. Developing the ability to learn from discriminating questions and the critical review of this learning allows for the correction of deviations from plans. If an organization is to truly respond to changes in the complex external environment, the possible *amplification* of such deviations is often helpful to create new products or services.

In so doing we begin to question other long-held assumptions of corporate life – those 'given' assumptions which are not given but simply accepted as the rules of the game – the 'industry formula'. Prime amongst the obstacles to creating effective Learning Organizations is the assumption that all budgets must span twelve months. While it is true that in most countries organizations have a legal duty to report to their owners and governmental authorities once a year, I have not come across a single country or company where it says that they have to do the same for their budgets. In a complex world twelve-month budgets are a nonsense – too long to cope with operational changes, and too short for strategic thinking. Yet we often base our whole planning round on this inappropriate time-frame. Different parts of an organization need different budgetary reporting periods so that they can learn effectively to keep their rate of change equal to, or greater than, the rate of change in their external environment.

It is curious to me that as more and more directors and managers accept that they must be increasingly nimble and responsive organizationally they still burden themselves with inflexible twelve-month budgets. This annual time-frame may be convenient for the accounts department to ensure the organization's legal duty of providing annual audited accounts, but accountants are not renowned for their user-friendliness, customer-orientation or imaginative thought processes. In companies that have broken with twelve-month budgets for many years – for example, Svenska Handelsbanken, the leading bank in Sweden and ABB (the Swedish-Swiss engineering multinational) – their rates of learning have increased rapidly and they have outperformed their market sectors. I have recently dealt with a major retail bank where the annual planning round takes up nearly eleven months of the year. The directors and managers are so exhausted by this that the twelfth month is spent on holiday recovering before they start again.

For anyone aspiring to create a Learning Organization the symbolic and practical power of destroying the obstacle of the annual budget mentality is worth investigating. It reinforces the idea that for effective Operational Learning it is essential for directors and senior executives to forget arbitrary rules and accept the delegation of power to the customer-facing staff, externally and internally, and so encourage them through action learning processes to learn regularly and rigorously from their daily work.

Ultimately it is the board and senior executives who create a positive, or negative, learning climate in their organization. They often do this unwittingly. However, they will be watched, eagle-eyed, by their staff to see if they really do 'walk the talk', or whether they say one thing but do another. If the latter, then over time the organization will slide into a blame culture and positive learning will falter, or stop. To prevent this the board must regularly monitor the organization's learning climate so that positive learning is rewarded as a key priority and organizational capability. A 'work smarter, not harder' organizational climate needs to be engendered by the board so that the staff move from, at worst, unconscious incompetence to, at best, conscious competence at the operational level of a Learning Organization.

This is a major challenge in itself and takes time and a commitment from the top to achieve. Yet in terms of the learning of the total organization it is necessary but not enough for a true Learning Organization. Sufficiency comes from integrating operational level learning at the policy formulation/foresight, and the strategic, levels of learning. To understand this we must start with Policy Learning.

# CHAPTER 4

# Policy Learning

If Operational Learning focuses mainly on increasing organizational efficiency, then Policy Learning focuses on increasing organizational effectiveness. The two opposing forces are then balanced by Strategic Learning.

Policy Learning is an often overlooked aspect of organizational learning. This is because it deals with wider, external political issues which are seen as above the remit of most managers and professionals. Policy Learning concerns the interface between the organization and its complex, external world. It is this world which provides the 'energy niches' in which the organization survives. This external environment is complex, unpredictable, fast-changing and full of risks. It is also full of customers, suppliers and other stakeholders such as politicians, legislators, regulators, community groups and environmental protection groups who can help build (or destroy) the organization.

It is the board of directors who are ultimately responsible for Policy Learning. Yet at any time many staff members are actively working in their operational learning roles in their external environment. A wise board recognizes this and builds them into informing and debating Policy Learning. They become an essential part of the upper loop of the 'triple-loop learning' process. As has been noted previously, without Policy Learning and its focus on the customer's perception of organizational effectiveness, it is too easy for directors to slip into an over-concentration on organizational efficiency and the downward spiral of 'downsizing and rightsizing' and inevitable capsizing.

*Policy* is a Greek derived word which entered the English language originally with a 't' rather than the modern 'c' – polity. It is the highest level of organizational learning, sitting above the levels of Strategic and Operational Learning. It is concerned with the organization's changing relationships with its external world so as to ensure its energy niches, and hence its survival. Policy Learning is about maintaining, developing, or changing the organization's 'political' relationships with those parties that directly or indirectly influence its information-gathering, risk-assessment and decision-making processes. Policy is not about the rules and procedures that govern an organization – whether this is who can spend what money, or who gets to park their car where – sadly this is how the word 'Policy' is still often taught at many business schools and used in many organizations.

Policy needs much deeper, imaginative, sustained and values-based thinking processes by the direction-givers than either Strategic or Operational Learning. Indeed Policy Learning is an exercise of the individual and corporate brain which demands levels of intellectual subtlety that often frighten off executives who have only been successful at operational thinking and learning. Policy Learning demands additional competence development for most executives. Many balk at having to retrain at what they thought was the comfortable end of a long and successful career. Yet the modern world demands that directors are assessed as competent external risk-assessors and direction-givers. How does one cope with this?

Policy Learning has two key elements:

- processes for maintaining and developing the energy and emotional climate of the organization so that its people are committed to it and are willing to learn with it
- processes for monitoring and sensing continuously the organization's changing external environment

While the second will make sense to all managers and directors the first is more difficult for the 'rationalist' executives to accept. The basic argument is that all work has two elements – task and process – and if this latter 'social-emotional' process is not taken into account, both the individual and the organization will underperform the task. Many executives see any time spent on the social process as a sign of 'softness'. Yet learning negative things in an organization is as important a process as learning positive things. Unless staff are encouraged to drive the organization forward constructively – being 'e-motional' – even the most rational of tasks has a high probability of having obstacles put in its way.

## PURPOSE, VISION AND MISSION

An organization is carried forward by the emotional, mental and physical energies which its staff are willing to give to it. The main sources of e-motional energy throughout an organization are initially generated at the policy level by the board. Ensuring that the board's words are seen by the staff to be in synchronization with their actions is a key duty for them. The board is watched continuously by the staff and any differences between words and actions will go around the informal grapevine of the organization. People will believe the truth of the actions rather than the words.

I have found many executives genuinely puzzled by the loose usage of three words – 'purpose', 'vision' and 'mission'. They are misused frequently but they do have precise meanings and unless understood they are an obstacle to learning. *Purpose* describes the fundamental reason for which the organization exists. This is decided by the shareholders and their agents, the board. The purpose could be 'to sustain and develop the wealth of the family owners', or 'to create health gain for this region', or 'to create shareholder value'. A statement of purpose can be as short as Microsoft's 'a personal computer on every desk in every house' or as long as IBM's 'we shall increase the pace of change. Market-driven quality is our aim. It means listening and responding more sensitively to our customers. It means eliminating defects and errors, speeding up all our processes, measuring everything we do against a common standard, and involving employees totally in our aims.'

Such statements are not a new phenomenon. Since 1754 the Royal Society of Arts in London has thrived on 'The encouragement of arts, manufactures and commerce, in Great Britain, by bestowing rewards, from time to time, for such productions, inventions, or improvements as shall tend to the employing of the poor, to the increase of trade, and to the riches and honour of this kingdom by promoting industry and emulation.' Whatever the organization's purpose its phrasing often gives great insight into the nature of its values and its emotional climate. A statement of purpose is the bedrock of the organization. It is by definition impossible to achieve in the short-term.

A *vision* is a picture of how the organization could be far into the future, if the organization is to achieve its purpose. It is a picture to inspire people inside and outside the organization to strive for their purpose. It is designed to capture, stretch and motivate the imagination, e-motional energy and commitment of staff and customers by showing just how good things will be if everyone strives long and hard to achieve the purpose. Visions must not be easy to reach. In fact I argue that visions should be almost impossible to reach.

I have a client in the pharmaceutical industry whose vision is 'to become the world's first "green" pharmaceutical company'. They have lots of missions and projects to put as many pieces of the jigsaw together as possible – researching the rainforests, and investigating Chinese and Japanese herbal medicines to derive new natural chemical compounds – while coping with charges of bio-piracy from many newly emergent market economies and environmental groups. Their vision energizes their staff long-term. They do not have a single masterplan as they do not know what they will find, or how the external political environment will change. So they use contingent strategies and learn from them. Everyone knows that this vision will need a twenty to fifty year time-frame. They recognize that they will still have to deliver improving 'bottom-line' performance to satisfy the shareholders but the vision gives everyone a higher order goal at which to aim.

Visions focus people's energies and aspirations. The regional health authority's seemingly bland purpose – 'to create health gain for this region' – is insufficient to create energy and commitment. However, when seen in the context of its vision – 'to ensure a healthy life and a dignified death for the people of our region' – it has created a great deal of energy, controversy, public debate, and commitment amongst its staff.

The problem I find is that many directors and senior executives are not very imaginative and so prefer to deal with the immediate rather than seriously consider the future. We are facing an old issue which Schopenhauer pithily stated as 'most men see the limits of their own vision as the limits of the world'. Seriously facing the issue of the organization's vision can release undreamed-of energy in people.

A *mission* statement is a more easily achievable target or objective. Missions are achievable within short to medium-term time-frames. A mission has measurable outcomes: for example, increases in market share, volume growth or profitability within the scarce resources of funds, people and time. Missions are essentially an Operational Learning concept.

## Values

Purpose and vision set the intellectual framework for the organization to face its future. Significant energy is released to achieve the vision if the board is clear about the values to which they, and the staff, subscribe. A value is a belief in action. Many boards of directors will quickly cobble together, endorse and declaim a 'values statement'. But there is little learning because they then usually dump the statement on the staff without explanation or consultation. The staff treat the exercise with open cynicism and use the printed statements as dart boards, or worse. They have no commitment to them. Such values statements will inevitably include 'customer satisfaction', 'business excellence', 'honest dealing', 'shareholder satisfaction', etc.

All of these are worthy in themselves but values need careful testing with staff and customers to ensure that they are true of the specific organization before they are promulgated. Sadly this step is often missed by directors, and scepticism or cynicism sets in amongst the staff. This is avoided by asking three simple questions before agreeing the detailed values:

• Is this value true of our organization?
• If so, how is each value to be benchmarked?
• How will each value be built into behaviours to be measured in the appraisal system for all staff, including directors?

Unless these questions are dealt with transparently by the directors and senior managers a values statement will have little credibility, however nicely wrought. Credibility is built by ensuring that the corporate appraisal system is designed so that at least 50 per cent focuses on, and rewards, values-based behaviours. This puts across the strong message that in this organization you are rewarded not just for *what* you achieved (the delivery of the task) but also for *how* you achieved it (the values-based behaviour) – and that both aspects are of equal importance for the long-term survival of the organization. Each value selected and tested by the board must be capable of being described by two or three observable and measurable behaviours which are then integrated into the appraisal system. In this way staff can be encouraged to show accountability, transparency and probity across their organization because everyone is appraised with the same values regardless of the tasks they perform.

I have recently facilitated the development of such a values-based appraisal system across a financial services company of some 100,000 people. Having been involved with the initial design I then monitored progress and came back at the very end as the upward-appraisals reached the top team and moved towards the chairman. Few in the organization believed that 'the old man' would participate in this 'values-based stuff' as he had a very successful career behind him, driven by relatively autocratic behaviour, and they thought that he was unlikely to be swayed by such a 'soft' process. However, he was keen to participate and received what he saw as helpful peer assessment by fellow directors and upward feedback from his eleven direct reports. His fellow directors were seriously worried about giving this feedback (even though it was anonymous) but found the process constructive once the ice was broken. The chairman even published a small article about his experience in the staff journal. This had a noticeably energizing effect on the staff and greatly boosted the credibility of the appraisal process. In its own small way it has also been a step forward for democracy at work.

However, there is though a 'shadow side' to values. If the production of a values statement is treated as a *fait accompli* and never put to the test, then it can seriously block critical review and organizational learning. It can create a negative learning climate where people learn things that kill the development of the organization. For example, in another financial services company the board declared 'honesty' as a core value. To their annoyance I insisted that we check each declared value against a sample of staff's perceptions before we went public. To their horror they found that their staff did not rate them as an honest organization. This was not to say that they were venal, rather that they had developed systems over many years where any risk to the bank failed-safe on their side. Over time this had created an anti-customer culture where the 'punters' could never win. Figures were rounded up in favour of the bank, customers were not told of better deals than their present accounts, money transfers were credited on average two days later than other companies. The board were genuinely shocked by their staff's perception and a major rethink is under way about the way they handle the minutiae of customers' transactions. They realize that if 'honesty' is to be a core value, then they have a lot of work to do in adapting their procedures and value sets.

## Organizational Climate and Culture

The combination of the emotional effect on staff of purpose, vision and values creates the organization's emotional climate – its preparedness to learn positively or negatively. Over time this emotional climate creates the symbols and acceptable behaviours that form the organization's 'culture'. Both emotional climate and organizational culture are measurable. Indeed, both need benchmarking and regular measurement to ensure that the organization has the competence to achieve its purpose. A values-based appraisal system helps generate the necessary positive emotional climate where people are seen to be rewarded not just by achieving their task but by doing it in a way that reinforces the organization's values.

As with values, there is also a 'shadow side' to the emotional climate of any organization. This comes to the fore when the directors, senior executives and line managers adopt an attitude of 'do as I say, not as I do'. Remember that staff watch executives attentively to see if they do 'walk the talk'. If not, then the staff will follow the executive's behaviours rather than their rhetoric. I was working with a board who had put a lot of time and money into improving the quality of the 'white goods' (refrigerators, cookers, etc.) they manufactured. All seemed to be going well until the last quarter of the year when quality fell off noticeably. One Friday afternoon the chief executive and I sat in his car outside the factory and randomly stopped the delivery lorries. We found that faulty goods (minor faults, but still faults) were being despatched despite all the TQM systems and executive rhetoric. On investigation we found that the managers were more concerned that they received their annual bonuses rather than ensured consistent quality. Annual bonuses were still awarded on mainly volume criteria. So this final part of an otherwise robust system had to be adjusted to ensure that quality was the dominant criterion for reward, while volume targets still had to be met.

Jaguar Cars' new manufacturing plant at Coventry is a good example of a significant change of culture in a relatively short time. The circular production line has inter-acting teams working to complete a high-quality premium-priced product. The workers have agreed among themselves, and with trade union agreement, that any team or team member delivering substandard work can be disciplined without direct reference to management. They are a set of essentially self-managing workgroups. This is a good example of 'culture' being defined by the workgroups at its simplest level as 'the way we do things around here'. From this the accumulated knowledge, attitudes and skills lead to the symbols and acceptable behaviours that give truth to the saying 'Man is an animal suspended in webs of signification he himself has spun'[32]. It is the board of directors' role to learn how to make these webs as constructively critical as possible.

## THE 'HEART OF THE ORGANIZATION'

The cumulative effect, positive or negative, of the board's Policy Learning in the fields of purpose, vision, values, emotional climate and corporate culture is to create 'the heart of the organization'. This embodies the core values and focus which generate energy to power the whole organization. Some organizations are vibrant, others seem to have no energy at all. It is the amount of time the board spends creating such positive energy that generates continuing organizational learning and effectiveness. But the area of Policy Learning and creating the 'heart of the firm' is often missed entirely by boards. Such boards feel it inappropriate to talk about the 'emotional climate' of their organization rather as the Victorians refused to talk about sex. I predict that in the twenty-first century focus on generating and maintaining a positive emotional climate will become a key role for directors and executives, especially as knowledge management software takes over the more routine information processing aspects of their jobs.

## FORESIGHT

Purpose, vision, values and culture can be seen as the 'soft' side of Policy Learning. There is a need for a 'hard' side as well – ways of monitoring and assessing the risks coming from the changing external environment. Returning to the original meaning of the word 'policy' we are seeking ways for a board to become sensitive to the changing patterns of events outside the organization so that it can pursue its political purpose. From thoroughly studying these external changes the board has a much better chance than its competitors of effectively pursuing its 'political will'.

I am not arguing that boards should be able to foresee the future. That is inconceivable. However, I am arguing that boards should be so sensitized to the complex, changing external world that they can make rapid and informed responses to reset their course in the turbulent seas. They are called 'directors' for good reasons. They are charged above all with showing the way ahead and giving leadership.

How then does a director become sufficiently sensitized to be able to monitor and assess the changing environment? The simplest answer is 'with difficulty'. My work has shown that less than 10 per cent of those promoted to the job title of 'director' have this capacity. This is not because they are inherently stupid or indolent but because there is often organizational collusion, witting or unwitting, by a few top people to agree that directing is not a proper job in itself. So neither time nor budgets are made available to bring 'directors' to competence in their new role. The chairman's role in inducting, including, and ensuring competence for new directors is rarely acknowledged. This is crazy, because without conscious learning processes at board level, the very conditions in which the 'fish rots from the head' are created.

When boards ask me to work with them on developing policy thinking and learning skills they often suggest investing in all sorts of on-line, real-time electronic databases to do the external environmental monitoring. Such tools are fine – once you have learned the art of asking those discriminating questions needed to use the tools effectively. Otherwise we are back to the classic 'garbage in, garbage out' process. The key is in turning directors' thinking from a 'convergent' style (as needed in management) to a 'divergent' one which is capable of scanning diverse data without having to focus immediately on to a single problem and then solve it. This sounds so strange to many directors that they feel uncomfortable and often demand the rapid installation of the electronic systems.

So I ask 'would you be willing to pay £10 a week for each board member to be able to effectively monitor the environment?' The figure is so low that it is usually treated with ridicule, especially when they are about to spend hundreds of thousands of dollars on new electronic systems. Yet for this modest sum directors and executives can easily have skilfully designed information on their desk. It comes in the form of daily broadsheet newspapers and weekly news magazines. They are encouraged to read these at their desks as the start of their direction-giving day. Whether they choose to read for example the *Financial Times*, the *Wall Street Journal*, Le Monde, or the *South China Morning Post* each day, or *The Economist* or *Newsweek* or *Asia Week* weekly is up to them. The important thing is that they learn the personal discipline, and benefits, of daily reading to scan the changing external environment.

Such a notion often creates adverse reactions along the lines of 'we just do not have enough time to do that' or 'what if we are caught reading at work? . . . we have to do that stuff at home'. Both questions say a lot about the lack of a directorial culture in such organizations. Unless directors budget significant and regular time to scan, critically review, debate and risk assess the changing external environment, then there is little hope of them coping with Policy Learning. Their role is to think effectively about the evolving future and then to direct others to take action, to execute proposals. We seem to have developed a managerial and professional world that values action, or at least being seen to be busy, above all. This is debilitating when coping with Policy Learning.

In developing boards of directors I persist with the daily newspaper idea. For those too intimidated to openly read at their desks, these texts are also available on computer screens via the Internet. But this does not make the same symbolic point to others that directing is a job which legitimately requires the directorial processes of scanning and reflection – and that these skills have to be learned. Even for existing and potential director development processes in major banks I have had to bring in newspaper editors to teach short, and very private, courses on how a newspaper is laid out and to address the issue of letting them learn *everything I wanted to ask about the* Financial Times *but never dared ask for fear of looking foolish*. It is often remarkable what has not been learned in a managerial or professional career, and how liberating it is to be able to say so and rectify matters. Once you understand the categories that form a newspaper, and read it regularly, it is surprising how quickly one can scan, and become sensitized to, the changing environment.

I use a simple categorization in the early stages of board development for Policy Learning based on the 'PPESTT' analysis. It is looking for changes in the:

- Political environment
- Physical environment
- Economic environment
- Social environment
- Technological environment
- Trade environment

Each of these can be broken down into sub-categories, for example:

The Political Environment

- understanding the broad policies and actions of the main political parties in the countries in which you operate, watching for changes and tracking forthcoming elections

The Physical Environment

- monitoring the national and global debates on the pollution of the environment and tracking new, or proposed, regulations which could affect your operations (e.g., transportation of goods or packaging disposal laws) or your future strategy (health and legislative pressure on e.g., smoking, use of cars, drinking alcohol, use of nuclear power, etc.)

The Economic Environment

- monitoring the politicians' handling of regional, national and international economies and the likely consequences of their behaviours – checking that their political rhetoric is in line with their behaviours, and building alliances where necessary

The Social Environment

- monitoring the demographic trends in the countries in which you operate
- monitoring the life-style trends among your customers and consumers
- monitoring fast changing fashion trends
- identifying new social groupings

The Technological Environment

- monitoring the evolution of new technologies, and new designs
- tracking the debates on the likely consequences of such developments
- identifying new market segments

The Trade Environment

- tracking regional and national trade trends
- tracking international trade trends between the 'global blocs' – US, EU and East Asia
- monitoring the World Trade Organization's decisions to help predict world trade flow trends

Written out like this the list can look intimidating enough to send a director straight back to micro-managing the operations instead. I would not expect any individual to be able to handle all these portfolios at once. I tend to use a 'buddy system' pairing two diverse directors (ideally an independent and an executive), or a director and a senior executive seen as a potential director, to take just one of these aspects as their 'policy portfolio' for a period of three months. They then report back their findings at special quarterly Policy Learning meetings, and then hand the portfolio to another pair as they in turn take up a new one. Over a period of around eighteen months the ability of the board to work at policy level increases enormously – and their reliance on a single specialist individual to always comment on 'their' functional area decreases. Remember that a board of directors is charged with taking collective decisions on behalf of the future of their organization. Their ability to fight the 'techno-babble' of functional specialists and so to take wise decisions is much improved by the collective critical debate.

Once these basic policy-formulating skills are learned then the board can move on to begin to integrate their Policy Learning with their strategic thinking skills through the development of 'scenarios'. These are not a prediction of the future, but pictures of possible futures on which the board can hone its direction-giving skills by debating how they would respond to such circumstances. In this way they are more informed and more ready to respond to disruptions from the environment than their competition. I will go into this in greater depth in the next chapter.

Although Policy Learning is the responsibility of the direction-givers they cannot be expected to do it alone – the field is so vast and they are so few. As mentioned at the start of this chapter, many staff members are out in the external world dealing with customers, suppliers and stakeholders. Some staff members will be also trade union officials, or local government councillors, or active in local charities. Information from all of these people can help fuel the Policy Learning debates. We are now seeing a significant shift by major organizations away from the fixation with the financial bottom-line. The idea of all organizations, private or public, being held accountable for 'triple bottom-lines' in the twenty-first century is beginning to take hold. A triple-bottom-line concerns simultaneous accountability for the financial, physical environmental, and social performance of the organization. John Elkington's excellent book *Cannibals with Forks*[33] gives many helpful examples of how this trend is developing.

It is vital to have as many externally aware staff as possible giving regular feedback of their learning and so contributing to the democratizing processes of critical review and debating policy-formulation. The integration of this learning takes us into the area of Strategic Learning to which we now turn.

# CHAPTER 5

# Strategic Learning

Strategic Learning focuses on the integration, risk-assessment, and balanced decision-making processes at the centre of the organization's learning. The output from Strategic Learning allows the board of directors and senior executives to both drive the organization forward and keep it under prudent control. Strategic Learning is the central processor of the organization – the organization's 'corporate brain' – bringing together, assessing and balancing information and ideas flowing from the external world of Policy Learning, and the internal world of Operational Learning. Moreover, it is the focus of the democratizing learning processes of any organization. It brings together and uses the learning from the board and the executives as well as from all of those customer-facing and community-facing staff who are learning through their day-to-day work for the organization.

## THE LEARNING BOARD MODEL

The *learning board* is the central processor of the three cycles of organizational learning – assessing risks and giving direction through ensuring a forum for critical review and debate – the 'parliament' of the business. The essential board model[34] is shown in Figure 19.

The Learning Board model is designed in quadrants defined by the two axes of focus (internal and external) and time-frame (short-term and long-term). This creates two defined areas of 'board performance' (driving the organization forward) both of which are concerned with the long-term – policy formulation and foresight, and strategic thinking – plus two areas of 'board con-

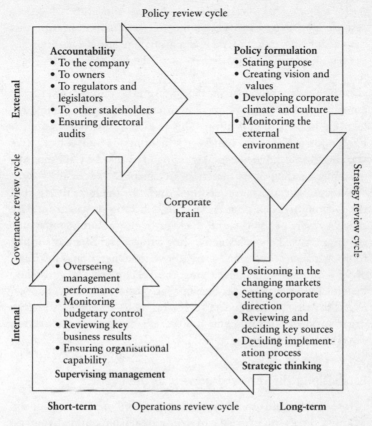

Figure 19 The Learning Board model

formance' (ensuring prudent control) both of which are short-term – management supervision and accountability. It is a fractal of the Learning Organization model's two aspects of 'organizational effectiveness' (driving forward) and 'organizational efficiency' (ensuring careful control).

An effective board of directors must be competent at integrating all four sections. The present focus of the new field of 'corporate governance' has tended to be on board conformance and regulatory issues only, while the growing demand of owners and stakeholders has been for assessing board competence and performance. This has led to a skewed allocation of scarce resources by many boards in favour of conformance. In turn, this has meant that much of their integrative Strategic Learning has been underplayed, to the detriment of the business and its long-term survival.

It should be stressed again that board attitudes, words and the competence of their subsequent actions determine the climate for learning in their organization. This is easy to say, but it is much harder for a board to achieve the continuous and constructive learning that it advocates. This is mainly caused by the board's misunderstanding of its direction-giving role.

Direction-givers are frequently seduced by the lures of crises in the Operational Learning cycle. This is because it was from here that they were promoted, they feel very happy about going 'hands on' in a crisis. This is seductive but wrong. The director's job is to budget significant time to rise above the Operational Learning cycle – adopting and developing the helicopter view – to look beyond the immediate problems, sense the future as it changes, assess the risks, and allocate scarce resources to best achieve the organization's purpose. This is a basic statement of the process of strategic thinking.

## Establishing the reserved powers of the board

Before rushing into the joys of strategic thinking I should give a warning. From many years of consulting I have noted that no matter how keen a board of directors is to break out of its oper-ational shackles and take board performance seriously through benchmarking and regularly measuring progress, it usually ends in tears unless they have first agreed the 'reserved powers' of that board. Reserved powers define the level at which directors have the ultimate power to take key decisions on the strategic allocation of resources. This is crucial to clarifying which decisions must be taken by the board, and which by the managers. Reserved powers are the decisions that only the board can take on behalf of its owners. Figure 20 shows a typical list of reserved powers for a UK listed company. However, reserved powers apply just as much to public sector and non-profit-making organizations. Without them there is the continuing potential for confusion between directors and managers as to who has authority to take which decisions. This can lead to badly informed risk-assessment and decision-taking, little learning and so board under-performance. Clarity of reserved powers is fundamental to clarity of learning at the strategic level.

# A statement of a board's reserved powers from a large quoted public company

## Companies Act requirements

1   Approval of interim and final financial statements.
2   Approval of an interim dividend and recommendation of the final dividend.
3   Approval of any significant change in accounting policy.
4   Appointment or removal of the company secretary.
5   Remuneration of auditors and recommendations for appointment or removal of auditors.

## Stock exchange requirements

1   Approval of all circulars and listing particulars and approval of routine documents such as periodic circulars re scrip dividend procedures.
2   Approval of press releases concerning significant matters described by the board.

## Management

1   Approval of the group's commercial strategy.
2   Approval of the group's annual operating budget.
3   Approval of the group's annual capital expenditure plan.

4   Changes relating to the group's capital structure or its status as a plc.
5   Terms and conditions of employment of directors and their service agreements.
6   Major changes to the group's management and control structure.

## Board membership and board committees

1   Board appointments and removals.
2   Terms of reference of chairman, deputy chairman, chief executive, and other executive directors.
3   Terms of reference and membership of board committees.

## Cadbury recommendations

1   Major capital projects (projects in excess of £30 million).
2   Material contracts of the company or any subsidiary in the ordinary course of business, e.g. bank borrowing in excess of £25 million.
3   Contracts of the company or any subsidiary not in the course of ordinary business, e.g. loans and repayments above £25 million, foreign currency transactions above £25 million.
4   Major investments or disposals above £30 million or, if the monetary sum is less than £30 million, the acquisition or disposal of interests of more than 2% in the voting shares of any publicly-quoted company or the making of any takeover bid for any publicly-quoted company of whatsoever value.
5   Risk management strategy.
6   Treasury policies.

## Miscellaneous

1 Changes in the trustees or rules of the company pension scheme.
2 Changes in the rules of employee share schemes and the allocation and grant of employee share options.
3 Political donations.
4 Prosecution, defence, or settlement of litigation involving sums above £1 million or being otherwise material to the interests of the company.
5 Internal control arrangements.
6 Health and safety policy.
7 Environmental policy.
8 Directors' and officers' liability insurance.
9 Directors' interests in shares and share options.
10 Directors' external interests.
11 Use of common seal.

**Figure 20 An example of the reserved powers of a board**

The statement of reserved powers will vary from company to company.

## The broad framework for Strategic Learning

Strategic Learning cannot work effectively unless it is seen within the wider framework of the Learning Board.[34] I will restate the 'four dilemmas' for any board here as they are the basis of Strategic Learning:

- driving the organization forward while keeping it under prudent control
- being sufficiently knowledgeable about the workings of the organization to be answerable for its actions, yet being able to stand back from operations management to retain a more critical, objective, long-term view
- being sensitive to short-term, local issues and yet being

informed about broader international trends and competition
- being focused on the commercial needs of the organization whilst acting responsibly towards other stakeholders and the physical environment[35]

The Strategic Learning aspects of each dilemma are highlighted clearly as – driving the enterprise forward; standing back to take a more critical and objective longer-term view; being informed about broader international trends and competition; and acting responsibly towards other stakeholders and the physical environment. How many boards do you know that budget a significant amount of time for these issues? It is essential for a learning board to commit to its role as the 'corporate brain'.

To cope with these dilemmas it is necessary to break them down into tasks in which each competence, individual and collective, can then be assessed. The learning board model describes four directorial tasks:

- Policy formulation and foresight
- Strategic thinking
- Management supervision
- Accountability

These form a natural rhythm to a board's year. Each directorial task feeds into the next and so gives shape to the total direction-giving role. A learning board's year starts with checking that the purpose, vision and values are still appropriate. In a healthy organization they will change very slowly, if at all. But they still need to be measured to ensure their validity as benchmarks for assessing all the other learning inputs of the quadrant. In addition the emotional climate and culture of the organization need to be measured against previously agreed benchmarks to ensure that staff are still committed to the vision, and that the values are being rewarded appropriately through the appraisal system.

In learning terms there is an important process to start the strategic year. The initial board meeting needs to ensure that the environmental monitoring systems are in place and working well so that the information on the changing world can be fed from the policy aspect of 'monitoring the external environment' across the interface to the strategic thinking aspect of 'positioning in the changing market'. This is fundamental to effective Strategic Learning. The quality of the debate, risk assessments and decisions here determine the effectiveness of the board's annual cycle – and well beyond that.

The arrowhead between policy formulation and strategic thinking is highly significant. Yet from my research it is one of the two weakest aspects of directorial thinking and learning. I argue that the capacity of board members to think strategically, flexibly and to take hard decisions when there is never sufficient information around to be risk-free, defines an effective learning board. So the interplay around the arrowhead of 'monitoring the changing external environment' and 'positioning in the changing market' is the pivot of Strategic Learning. It is measurable, and must be closely monitored, if it is to be the integrator of the three learning cycles. It is from here that risks are assessed, direction given, scarce resources allocated and the implementation and feedback processes of strategy agreed. These tasks define the true role of the director as strategist.

I should stress that here I am talking of the competence of strategic thinking, not 'strategic planning'. I agree with Henry Mintzberg in his excellent book *The Rise and Fall of Strategic Planning*[36] that strategic planning is a contradiction in terms, an unhelpful oxymoron like 'fun run', 'friendly fire' and 'military intelligence'. I repeat that as far back as 1976 it was acknowledged by the then doyen of strategic planning, Igor Ansoff, that all was not well with the existing strategic planning process:

> over the past twenty years, it has become increasingly clear through lessons of success and failure, as well as through continuing research, that the Cartesian conception of the strategic problem suffers from two major deficiencies. First, in the language of management science, it is an 'improper optimisation' – the excluded variables have major impact on the preferred solution. Second, strategic planning solves only part of the total problem concerned with the maintenance of a viable and

effective relationship between the organization and the environment[37].

Many organizations using strategic planning have still not come to terms with this statement – so they waste valuable resources in ineffective strategic processes.

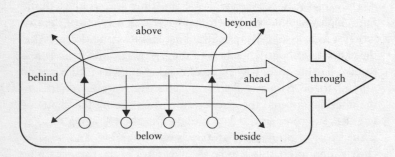

**Figure 21 Strategic thinking as seeing**

I find Mintzberg's 'strategic thinking as seeing' model[38] is helpful here to explain in one drawing what the board is setting out to learn.

Mintzberg argues that if you think strategically (and I would add consciously seek to balance the Operational and Policy Learning cycles) then the board's work is not only 'seeing ahead', it requires a further six competences. These are:

- seeing behind
- seeing above
- seeing below
- seeing beside
- seeing beyond
- seeing it through

It is essential that the board has the capability of *seeing behind* and understanding the historical roots from which the organization's present values have derived. Mintzberg quotes Kierkegaard – 'life may be lived forward, but it is understood backwards'.

He characterizes *seeing above* as finding the diamond in the rough. There is no readily available big picture for any strategist, each must construct their own.

Yet strategic thinking is inductive thinking – extending the particular into the general picture – so *seeing below* is equally important. One needs to be able to benchmark the present so that one can understand how far one still has to go to reach an objective or strive towards a vision. Strategic thinking is a creative process, searching for the gems and insights the others overlook as they pursue the accepted 'industry formula'.

*Seeing beside* is the 'thinking out-of-the-box' process to which so many now aspire – being sensitized to aspects of the changing environment, which may have no immediate connection to your organization, but which keep you in touch with the wider changes in society. It can be developed consciously by any board.

*Seeing beyond* signifies that creative ideas need to be positioned in a future context – to be located in a possible world that is yet to unfold. So more than just seeing ahead, seeing beyond sets out to create that new world.

Mintzberg then makes the fundamental point that none of this is worth doing unless you are capable of *seeing it through*. Unless conscious implementation and feedback processes are put in place by the board from the start, then effective Strategic Learning is not sustainable.

The competence of strategic thinking is rarely developed consciously by organizations for their existing (or potential) direction-givers. It needs to become a crucial part of their induction, inclusion and competence-building personal development process as they enter a board. Without competent strategic thinking in individuals – and the board as a whole – it is impossible to reach the 'board performance' indicators increasingly demanded and assessed by ever more critical owners. My *Developing Strategic Thinking* programmes at the Institute of Directors in London and Hong Kong, and at Imperial College, London, have proved increasingly popular as directors become aware of this need.

## STRATEGY IMPLEMENTATION

In the learning board model the arrowhead from 'deciding implementation processes' and 'reviewing key business results' defines the second of the major weaknesses in directors' thinking processes. The arrowhead signifies the interaction of two key learning objectives at the interface between board performance and board conformance – strategic thinking and management supervision. Yet, this is one of the most unpopular styles of leadership thinking for the vast majority of directors, as Jerry Rhodes' recent research shows[39]. The unpopularity of thinking seriously about the future, of preferring 'soft' to 'hard' data, and of playing down personal values and levels of commitment is very worrying. It suggests a disregard for the very competences that encourage board performance. Even when directorial time is spent grappling with the issue of how to cope with the evolving future, my experience has shown that directors will not be keen to hear the hard facts of the effects of implementing their strategies. The two-way feedback and continuous learning between strategic thinking and management supervision is crucial to the balance of organizational effectiveness and organizational efficiency. When this balance is missing the organization suffers major obstacles to its ability to learn at all three levels.

My consulting experience using the *Thinking Intentions Profile*[40] (a method of measuring effective intelligence) demonstrates that most people who become directors have little interest in thinking about implementation and *learning* from two-way feedback. Indeed many become upset when authentic feedback explains why their implementation processes have failed to work. Yet this is one of their prime tasks as direction-givers – as strategists. It is worth remembering that the word 'strategy' derives from the ancient Greek meaning 'the world of the military general'. In active terms this means 'the broad deployment of scarce resources to achieve purpose'. All organizations have scarce resources, most have clear purposes. It is the direction-giver's job to optimize these scarce resources to achieve purpose and continuously learn from this process. This is a competence in Strategic Learning which can and must be developed in all directors.

From the interplay of strategic thinking implementation and the analysis of key results we are moving on our annual rhythm deeper into the 'board conformance' aspects of the learning board. Board conformance means budgetary control, overseeing management performance and ensuring organizational capability. The trick here for effective directors is to raise these aspects of Operational Learning to a more strategic level for better critical review. Here the role for direction-givers is to review the operational trends and patterns, intervening directly only when there are significant deviations from plan, or major disruptions from the external environment.

It is the chairman's job to develop the board to competence. To do this well the chairman must ensure that the directors do not try, as they are often inclined, to micro-manage the organization from the boardroom. Ideally the critical review of operations should not take the board more than an hour a month even in a large corporation. Their major tasks are to formulate policy, think strategically, give direction and be ultimately accountable for the total performance of the organization. With the development of new software which throws up operational trends and patterns, and has 'prompt questions' and 'intelligent agents' designed into it, an hour a month should be both necessary and sufficient to cope with the supervision of management.

Around month nine in a financial year a learning board needs to take time out to check its many accountabilities. The board is accountable first to the company itself as a separate legal entity, which they hold in trust on behalf of future generations. Only then is it accountable to the owners. Politics, societal values and the law have (in many countries) changed accountabilities over the past twenty years – hence the new interest in 'the triple bottom-line'. The previous seemingly absolute autonomy of many boards of directors is constrained increasingly by boards being held more tightly accountable for their relations not just to shareholders but also to regulators and legislators, customers, staff and suppliers. Health and safety issues, community relationships and the protection of the physical environment also impact on the boards of directors of many companies. All of these are 'stakeholders' about whom the board must learn to think and behave in a strategic and integrative manner. In all of the many stakeholder roles the staff can play a major and continuous part in helping the Operational Learning system feeding back information on how the organization is performing in relation to its accountabilities.

In addition the board must produce the company's annual financial statement – to demonstrate the quality of its stewardship of the organization – and, in a growing number of countries, it must audit and publish its performance in relation to environmental pollution, and health and safety at work. A few cutting-edge organizations are starting to audit and publish their community involvement, and their generation of intellectual property, as we move towards the 'knowledge worker' society. Such audits ensure that the board conformance aspects are measured with increasing regularity and rigour and are more open to internal and external scrutiny. Democratization is seen at work quietly here.

So being a board member in the twenty-first century will be accepted as a proper job which demands that new and strategic competences are learned by the direction-givers. A directorship will no longer be viewed as a nice add-on to the end of a successful period as a manager or a professional. To reinforce this point, when I am developing a board I insist that the 'executive' directors are paid a separate director's fee for their directorial work and that personal development plans are agreed and appraised for all board members in their direction-giving role. This includes the chairman and chief executive. Such personal development plans stress the fact that Strategic and Policy Learning are distinct from operational competences and need to be assessed and rewarded separately.

## DEVELOPING STRATEGIC THOUGHT IN A LEARNING ORGANIZATION

Once the learning board is established as the organizational centre for external and internal environmental information processing, critical debate, risk assessment, and strategic decision-taking, the wider debate on strategies and the diffusion of strategic thinking throughout the organization can begin in earnest.

There are many effective ways of doing this which are explained in depth in both *The Fish Rots from the Head*[41] and *Developing Strategic Thought*.[42] However, it is worth sketching an outline here of a process for developing strategic thought which has worked well in many private and public organizations in many countries.

## SWOTS AND PPESTTS – THE BASIS OF ORGANIZATIONAL LEARNING

The Strategic Learning process starts and ends with the creation and updating of a SWOT analysis – reviewing the organization's strengths and weaknesses, opportunities and threats. This is the single sheet of paper from which the board ultimately sets its strategy in terms of risk assessments, direction and the subsequent deployment of scarce resources. The SWOT analysis is the benchmark against which the total performance of the organization is measured on a regular and rigorous basis so that conscious learning can be made manifest. I use a three-month board cycle for updating the SWOT analysis, unless there is a major disruption in the environment. The information needed to deal with strengths and weaknesses comes mainly from the internal board conformance-orientated management supervision figures and organizational capacity survey data. The information needed for describing the opportunities and threats comes from the regular processes for scanning the changing external environment and the changing stakeholder interests.

However, the most difficult information for many boards to acquire is not from the general external environment (the previously mentioned 'buddy' system for directors working on the PPESTT analysis should cope with this). The problem is more the acquisition of authentic 'competitor analysis' and details of their strategic thinking and competences. In both western and eastern societies there seems to be an emotional block against systematically collecting competitor intelligence. Yet one's customer-facing staff, suppliers, and especially customers themselves are giving this information continuously and freely. It is not wise to codify and study this systematically? A Learning Organization needs to develop systems for capturing and codifying this free data on competitors. Yet to establish such a system is often seen as moving into the shady areas of spying and industrial espionage. I do not mean it that way. Rather, it should be like the notion mentioned earlier of 'hearing the baby cry', of being so sensitized to the movements of competitors (and markets) that the board can quickly decide whether an alteration of plans or strategies is needed. In strategic thinking terms the board can rapidly remix its strategic decisions as to when to:

- advance
- retreat
- maintain its position
- make alliances
- withdraw

It is worth noting two things about this list of strategic choices. First, that in turbulent markets the option 'maintain its position' is neither energy-free, nor resource-free. Second, that 'making alliances' is not always against your existing competitors. The notion of 'co-opetition'[43] is a useful idea. For example, in Media Projects International we regularly compete with another firm for national and international projects. However, for a particularly large project in Singapore neither of us had sufficient resources on our own to tender. By combining our resources under a single-project contract we tendered, won, and have worked well together – yet we still compete on all other tenders. In a complex and turbulent world we have had to learn to become highly adaptive while at the same time maintaining our unique purpose, vision and values.

## LEARNING TO CLARIFY ORGANIZATIONAL STRENGTHS AND WEAKNESSES

To clarify the more internally-orientated aspects of the SWOT – strengths and weaknesses – one can use a number of analytical tools. For example, Michael Porter's Value Chain model[44] helps directors and strategists look much more analytically at the flow of work through the organization, and at its organizational structure and processes. Most importantly it allows directors to measure the strengths and weaknesses of an organization in comparison to known competitors by asking 'where do we add margin in relation to them?' Cool and thorough analysis using the value chain model can be uncomfortable for a board initially because often many cherished myths about the organization and its competition bite the dust. But in the longer-term it can help enormously with the reframing of the way one does business. Initially the analysis may simply reinforce the fact that there are few, if any, areas in which you add significant margin in relation to your competitors. In this case the learning is that you are likely to be slavishly following the 'industry formula' and, therefore, learning at a rate insufficient to stop you from becoming commoditized. Then the question is can your rate of learning be sufficient to either become a cost leader in your industry, or to so differentiate yourself that customers will recognize you as providing good value-for-money and, ideally, may also pay a premium price for your product or service? It is the time budgeted by the direction-givers to the careful analysis, critical review, debate and risk-assessment around your strengths and weaknesses which adds so much to Strategy Learning and the broad deployment of scarce resources to achieve your purpose. Clarity of strategies creates much more effective learning in the operational cycle.

## LEARNING TO CLARIFY OPPORTUNITIES AND THREATS

For the more externally-orientated 'opportunities and threats' side of the SWOT analysis one can use, for example, another Michael Porter tool – the Five Forces model[45]. This helps strategically reframe the dimensions of the changing nature of competition in your chosen markets. Specifically, it allows a board to review five key dimensions of competitiveness:

- the threat of new entrants (contrasted with the costs of entry and the barriers to entry)
- the threat of new products or services (contrasted with the costs of entry and the barriers to entry)
- the economic (bargaining) power of suppliers

- the economic (bargaining) power of customers
- the churning (repositioning) of existing competitors.

This list may well remind you that economics is called 'the dismal science' with good reason, the categories do sound negative. However, the tool does give boards a very good picture of the frequently changing environment to which they can ascribe probabilities as part of their risk-assessment process prior to their strategic decision-taking.

Tracking the broad picture of an organization's changing environment, and rebalancing the risks over time, can by rigorous learning build great competence in a board. This 'general knowledge' learning can be achieved simply by reading the daily and weekly newspapers and the trade and professional press, collecting competitors' press releases and technical literature, profits statements, annual accounts and by sensitive listening at conferences and trade exhibitions. The careful codification, and thoughtful regular debate, of this data by the board, executives and customer-facing staff can prove highly cost-effective and give significant competitive advantage.

The quarterly revision of all four aspects of the SWOT analysis provides valuable data to fuel the key Strategic Learning processes for a board. But how is it then turned into useful learning in the other parts of the organization?

## THE INTEGRATION OF STRATEGY LEARNING

A recent Booz Allen & Hamilton/Economist Intelligence Unit report[46] while looking at the effect of the Internet and e-commerce, identified seven 'megatrends' which they predict will strongly affect future business:

- new channels are revolutionizing sales and brand management
- the balance of power is moving towards the (increasingly well-informed) customer
- competition is increasing across all dimensions
- the pace of business is fundamentally accelerating
- companies are transforming into extended enterprises

- companies are re-evaluating how they and their traditional value chains will add value in future
- knowledge is becoming a key asset

These trends alone make the case for clarifying directors' roles and the reserved powers of the board so that they can time-budget to keep themselves focused firmly on Strategic and Policy Learning, if only to keep up with such changes in the external environment. If our Learning Organizations are to become complex, adaptive systems, capable of generating a rate of learning equal to, or greater than, the rate of environmental change, then we can no longer afford to let our direction-givers rely only on Operational Learning. Already too much 'downsizing and rightsizing' has led to unsatisfactory results in such major organizations as Marks & Spencer, BA and the BBC. It will get worse as we go into the new millennium. We need to learn our way out of such poor strategic thinking.

The Learning Organization sets out to integrate the three cycles of learning needed to be both necessary and sufficient to cope with being a complex adaptive system. The three key learning cycles are being accepted increasingly by organizations in the private and the public sectors. The learning board idea as the central processor of learning in a Learning Organization is already in use on three continents.

Two major new organizational benchmarking processes, both of which accept the necessity of continuous organizational learning, have appeared. These are often being used in parallel, or in tandem, with the three-cycle Learning Organization processes.

## THE EUROPEAN FOUNDATION FOR QUALITY MANAGEMENT'S 'BUSINESS EXCELLENCE' MODEL

This increasingly popular European model (Figure 22)[47] accepts the notion of key organizational inputs – 'enablers' – and outputs – 'results' – and has a rigorous self-referential benchmarking process. From these benchmarks progress can be measured and debated across the organization. It relies on horizontal as well as vertical information and learning flows. While no formal feedback loops are designed into the model it assumes these exist.

Indeed the arrows shown in Figure 22 are mine and not part of the original model. I want to make the basic point that in using this EFQM model thoughtful directors, managers and staff are striving to measure and learn from all aspects of their organization *and* the inter-relationships of these elements. The model is not simply reliant on financial measures. The growth of the EFQM business excellence model has been impressive and now a range of organizations use it, from large corporations to small businesses and professional practices, government departments and non-profit making organizations. The model allows them more informed debates and decision-taking through its conscious and rigorous strategic learning systems. The measurement of the satisfaction levels of customers, staff, and society are a great step forward from most financially-orientated performance models and reinforce my work on organizational capabilities.

## THE BALANCED SCORECARD

An alternative, and US, model is the balanced scorecard[48]. This is a direct challenge to the long-prevailing anti-shareholder credo of Berle and Means[49] which in *The Modern Corporation and Private Property* (1933) stated that:

> 'in the Darwinian struggle for survival the American public company is the winner because of its reliance on the largely unfettered power of strong managers and the existence of small, fragmented shareholders weakened by their own inability to co-ordinate. If the shareholders do not like the use and abuse of this managerial power they can sell. This structure is seen as far outweighing in efficiency the costs that it incurs.'

This long-held acceptance of the abuse of managerial power is changing, even in the US, as at the extremes it leads to telephone number salaries and stock options for top executives without their delivering outstanding performance; and in addition the disillusioned shareholders (even those with few shares) are beginning to co-ordinate, especially through the Internet, and are arranging proxy votes to change top executives. Again we begin to see

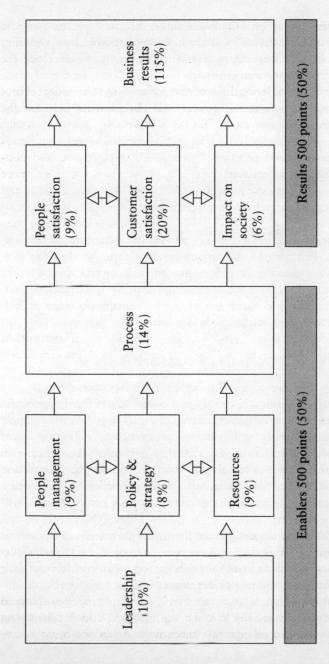

**Figure 22** The EFQM business excellence model

Enablers 500 points (50%)

Results 500 points (50%)

Leadership (10%)

People management (9%)

Policy & strategy (8%)

Resources (9%)

Process (14%)

People satisfaction (9%)

Customer satisfaction (20%)

Impact on society (6%)

Business results (115%)

another aspect of organizational democracy evolving. These 'shareholder activists' and their *Xcompanysucks.com* web-sites are currently learning at a rate equal to, or faster than, the underperforming executives.

The balanced scorecard helps greatly as it signals the importance of ensuring balanced organizational development between the countervailing forces of:

- Customer perspective
- Financial perspective
- Internal business perspective
- Innovation and learning perspective

Notice that 'learning' is a key part of the balancing mechanism. Again, benchmarks and targets are set so that the learning processes can measure the differentials and so keep redeploying scarce resources to achieve the strategic intent of the organization. Continuous strategic learning is at work to ensure the dynamic balances necessary at any point in time.

## THE CENTRAL PROCESSES OF STRATEGIC LEARNING

I argue that everyone in an organization has both the right, and the duty, to learn consciously and continuously from their work. Indeed, as I have suggested the right to learn may become accepted as a basic human right in the twenty-first century. It is the board of directors' role to ensure that they encourage their executives to create a positive learning climate throughout the organization so that all staff may contribute and be rewarded for so doing.

A learning board has as its central activity the continuous balancing of Revans' axiom – $L \geq C$ – as it drives the annual rhythm of its Strategic Learning cycle. It must create a series of continuing strategic debates with the owners, managers, staff and stakeholders so that it is as sensitized as possible both to changing environments and to its own organizational capabilities.

These strategic debates are the regular and rigorous 'critical reviews' at the organizational integration level. Such debates can range from General Electric's 'town meetings' to BP Amoco's intranet home page for all staff. They are the vital central processes of a Learning Organization as it grapples with the dilemmas and complexity of its learning in relation to the environment. It is trying to resolve each strategic dilemma in real time, while accepting that the process is infinite. One cannot truly 'resolve' problems for any length of time in a turbulent environment. One can only decide on how best to balance organizational effectiveness and organizational efficiency this time around. In addition the board is seeking to enhance the organization's asset base through the creation, and protection of its learning, made manifest through its generation of intellectual property. With the growth of the Internet and e-commerce this is going to be a tough but necessary role.

These strategic challenges for an aspiring Learning Organization may seem daunting. They certainly take us well beyond most people's view that 'learning' is only operational. Opening up the organization to more transparent learning, particularly horizontal learning across co-operating workgroups releases energy in the staff, and other stakeholders, to pursue the vision in remarkable and often unpredictable ways.

Some years ago I was a consultant for a large manufacturer of car tyres. The company was in dire straits and it looked as though we would have to close it down. The owners gave us a year to rescue it and once we made it public that our jobs were on the line just as much as the staff's, and that we could only resolve the problems with the active participation of the staff, things improved. It only took some ten weeks before most of the old restrictive practices were quietly abandoned by the staff themselves. The trade unions were officially opposed to us, but unofficially they backed us strongly because they saw we provided at least a ray of hope. Within eighteen months the company had learned to transform itself using self-managed action learning groups. Ironically it became the only profitable part of the then ailing group structure and was later sold at a good price to a willing buyer.

Handling such learning at the strategic level is often a novel challenge for the directors of a Learning Organization – and, as we shall see in the next chapter, this involves a serious reconsideration of how we employ people and encourage their active participation in an organization.

# CHAPTER 6

# Towards More Democratic Organizations

A Learning Organization has a higher chance of survival and development in a turbulent world than other organizations. Yet it takes some years to ensure that learning at the policy, strategy, and operational levels is fully established and integrated in such a way as to ensure the full participation of staff and other stakeholders. The word 'participation' can still cause major blockages to organizational learning. It derives from a Latin root with two distinct, yet linked, meanings. Participation means both 'joint responsibility' and 'joint ownership'. Sadly this potentially liberating idea has become stuck in a time-warp of 1960s politics. Many directors and executives encourage 'participation' when they mean their staff must accept more joint responsibility for their actions. Conversely, many trade unionists say 'participation' when they still mean only 'joint ownership'. As we move into the twenty-first century we will only see true Learning Organizations if both sides accept the word with both of its meanings – this is beginning to happen.

At present there are relatively few adventurous organizations actively seeking to take organizational learning theory and practice forward. Those organizations that are pushing at the boundaries of learning accept the integration of the three levels of learning as necessary as a process and then seek sufficiency in finding creative measures to ensure their staff's understanding, acceptance and commitment to continuous learning and development.

New experimental work on organizational learning is coming from two major sources. First, the more rigorous measurement of the integration of organizational and individual learning, and its effects on the total performance of the organization. Second, the growing awareness of the importance of ensuring competitiveness through gaining assets and creating value through codifying and diffusing continuous learning.

Both assume that people are the key to organizational learning – indeed that people are the *only* organizational resource that can learn – and that they need to be accepted increasingly by directors and senior executives as more of a key part of the critical review and debate processes within their organizations than at present. To achieve this happy state we need to think in a more democratic manner about the nature of the relationships between employers and employees, owners and their agents.

## LEARNING ACQUISITION, DEVELOPMENT AND MEASUREMENT

### A) Learning and employment contracts

Referring back to his recent book *Knowledge Assets*,[50] Max Boisot makes the profound point that if we are truly entering the 'age of the knowledge worker', and recognizing the importance of knowledge creation and management, then we are faced with a new phenomenon in industrial society – people are their own tools. This idea defines the break from the old 'industrial society' to the Information Age. Its effects are awesome, in terms of its political, social, economic and organizational consequences. This results in speeding up the democratization processes in organizations. The old Henry Ford complaint that 'when I hire a pair of hands, I get a person as well' is giving way to the increasing realization that 'when I hire a pair of hands I get a free brain as well'. This in turn gives rise to intense questioning in many organizations about how to value people at work. 'Value' here is used both in the senses of pricing and of beliefs. If you value people's learning as an organizational asset and declare employees as assets on your balance sheet (especially in the form of their creation of intellectual property) then you have a partial solution to the question. But you cannot bolt people to the floor and then depreciate them as you can machines. If dissatisfied they will leave – taking their knowledge and their ability to learn with them.

At present we are not organized to treat people as key assets, despite the chairman's annual rhetoric that 'our people are our biggest asset'. If this were true, where do they appear on the balance sheet? Perhaps this is also a clue? Are we moving (however hesitantly) away from the idea that 'learning equals training' and that it should be consequently a cost on the profit and loss account, towards a time when directors and owners will accept that 'our' people's learning is an asset generated by their creation, codification and diffusion of their knowledge, attitudes, values and skills? If so, then learning is likely to become the only sustainable asset of an organization in the new century. So learning must appear on the balance sheet.

At this point many accountants will turn red-faced and splutter. But accountants are not, and have not needed to be, famed for their fast rate of learning related to rapid societal change. They are more conformist, applying the rules during or after the event. But if they think about it, then the reflection of knowledge workers as assets on a balance sheet already exists, albeit in fairly exotic ways at present. Footballers are valued and traded as assets by their clubs as Arsenal and Manchester United demonstrate. So are pop stars and the copyright of their songs. Is the intellectual property created through learning in the organization to be made manifest in products, services and brands in future? 'Real' industrialists in production-orientated industries may scoff at such 'soft' attitudes as people as assets, but even their staff learn continuously both good and bad things about their organization. Such conscious and shared learning would help their organization be able to differentiate better and so avoid the very commoditization processes to which so much of the manufacturing and service industries are prone. But to do so would mean having to pay more attention to their staff's learning. The conscious acquisition, codification and diffusion of knowledge will be the processes that transform creative and developing organizations in the new millennium. Can any of us afford to scoff at such learning?

What if these predictions prove true? We would then need to

carefully consider our use, and frequent abuse, of our people's learning. As I have shown in the Policy and Operational Learning chapters our staff are learning good and bad things continuously. How do we as directors and managers capture the positives and reduce the negatives? Part of the answer is to create a 'learning climate' that encourages learning through constructive criticism and review as a norm and most importantly, seeks to avoid generating the corrosive 'blame culture'. Here the establishment of clear organizational purpose, vision and especially, transparent values-based behaviours and appraisal is a must.

Valuing people at work necessitates rethinking the basis of the employment contract. The previously universal, simple 'contracted hours' basis of time-for-money will need to be balanced by an 'emotional contract' as well. This means a move away from the legalistic idea of just turning up, doing the work to the minimum specifications for the contracted time, then going home and being paid at the end of the month. Twenty-first-century employment contracts will specify job performance requirements, not necessarily hours, and also the guaranteed developmental processes for the individual within and outside the organization. The emotional side of the contract will allow both technical training to do the job competently, an hours and money budget for developing personal competence within the organization, and an hours and money budget to ensure the individual's continuing 'employability' outside the organization. In a turbulent world where one cannot guarantee staff employment for long periods this latter condition is essential to maintain and motivate employees to add value in the short and medium term. This means developing an individual learning contract. I have argued this case in detail in *The Twelve Organizational Capabilities* so I will only mention two key elements here.

First, that any staff member (with their line manager) is expected as part of their employment contract to review regularly the effectiveness and efficiency issues of their part of the organization, and to implement improvements so that they and others, can learn from them. Staff need to accept, commit to and be rewarded for, not just the improvement to the internal workings of their unit but, just as importantly, to the relationships *between* their unit and other units – the horizontal learning processes. This is where significant value can be added, or lost, both economically and socially. Carefully selected diverse action learning groups can have a great impact on rapidly learning how to add such value.

Second, that employment contracts have both a legal and an emotional element to them. In Western societies part of the emotional employment contract acknowledges that a person's *learning* is energized by their recognition by the organization as an individual with development potential. So an employment contract for a 'knowledge worker' would state honestly that 'we cannot employ you for a lifetime, however if you deliver what we need on the "hard" task performance side, then we will make your job as interesting as we can and we will budget time and money to help you ensure your continuing employability in the outside job market'. This may sound simplistic but its clarity does generate a lot of goodwill and energy, provided that this side of the deal is delivered. Where such new employment contracts have been launched I have been pleasantly surprised by how well they have been received, and how much organizational and individual learning and development has been generated – often way beyond any reasonable expectation on the manager's side of what their investment would bring.

Workers in one engineering plant are offered a time-and-money budget of £400 and five working days a year for purely personal 'employability' development as part of their new employment contract. This is on top of their usual training budgets. A surprisingly large number have signed up for long-term distance learning programmes, often at degree level. This was not expected by the managers. The difference between the money and time the company offers and the full cost of the programmes is paid willingly by the staff. The enthusiasm and energy generated has been infectious and has led to the company establishing on-site 'learning centres' where both in-company and personal learning is encouraged.

Similarly, in an insurance company, and in a mortgage company, both of which were being closed down, the demotivated staffs were offered this new type of employment contract, in a desperate attempt to be good to staff during the run-down process. Many staff saw quickly that for young, and under-qualified people, and for the over-50s who thought that they were on the employment scrapheap, the chances for rapid development and promotion were much higher than in other companies. Quite rapidly the companies became known in their industries as 'training companies' for such people. Development for employability after the company closures generated a surprisingly positive and co-operative learning climate in the companies concerned – so much so that the businesses were turned round, became very profitable, and each was eventually reopened to new business – with highly capable, motivated staff and a demographically unusual profile.

Some companies are taking the notion of linking learning and employability further. Motorola, Unipart, British Airways, and Lloyds TSB among others have created 'corporate universities' to foster and encourage such trends. These offer personal development to all levels of the organization, allowing people to seek personal recognition and advancement while also fulfilling basic training needs. In an age of 'knowledge workers' this approach is crucial for an organization to survive. Remember that the word 'development' derives from the Latin 'volupe' and means 'seeing the richness within; and making it manifest'. This is the powerful basis of the emotional side of the employment and learning contract. It is of key importance to organizations where people are their own tools. It also cheers me up to think that here we are dealing with issues of the voluptuousness of human potential, rather than just the legalese of contracts and the prosaic 'bottom-line'.

## B) Intellectual property

However, there is also a growing 'hard' edge to the consequences of individual and organizational learning. If people are our biggest asset, then we need to reframe many of our organizational values in relation to them. We invest in assets. We maintain assets. We depreciate assets, and we budget to replace them. How many of these do you do systematically in relation to your employees and their learning?

Those organizations that are seeking to invest in and capitalize on organizational learning are seeking specifically to establish a legal property right over the outputs from their staff's learning.

They then seek to protect that legal right as an asset. This is precisely where 'learning' can leave the cost side of the profit and loss account and move to the balance sheet. At the integrative, strategic level of learning the implications of this are profound. It is very likely that in the twenty-first century the old mindset that assets can only comprise land, labour and capital will be overtaken by a new mindset, of people, learning and capital. The physical 'dematerialization' of business and government is already under way, and the rapid growth of cyber-space is fuelling this process. So the creation and protection of intellectual property – 'know-how' and 'know-why' – is likely to become an organizational meta-competence in the twenty-first century.

The World Trade Organization already recognizes five main categories of intellectual property:

- Patent
- Copyright
- Registered design
- Trademark
- Servicemark

In some countries these are supplemented by the legal notion of 'trade secrets'. Many industries already run on the foundation of intellectual property. For example, the pharmaceutical industry is patent-driven. Software writing and publishing are copyright-driven. Design is registered-design driven. Retailing is trademark (and brand) driven. Service industries are servicemark-driven. Each industry is seeking to establish and protect its investment in learning. Some are now realizing that this is not just important for the physical and legal manifestation of that learning, but also for the effectiveness of the organizational processes and capabilities which generate effective individual, workgroup and ultimately organizational learning. To capitalize on this learning in future people will need to be treated more democratically – as an essential part of the total organizational learning process. They will need to be better informed to be able to participate in making more conscious and discriminating organizational choices. This all sounds very noble. Let us hope that this is how we will progress.

However, there are counter-arguments which demonstrate the 'shadow side' of the intellectual property idea. Many of these issues show the natural inclination of businesses to try to create monopolies, and to defeat the attempts by governments and customers to stop this. At present the issue of genetically modified (GM) crops clearly highlights some of the issues involved. Some bio-technology companies are creating crops which have definite economic cost advantages for farmers in the western economies; they also have a downside – definite, or potential disadvantages for customers, the physical environment and possibly society as a whole. The companies taking the brunt of this criticism at the time of writing are Monsanto, Dupont and Novartis. The arguments against them range from the curtailment of consumer choice: the unknown effects, short and long term, of such genetic engineering on both the physical environment and the human body; and the exploitation of poor farmers in the developing world through the creation of 'terminator genes' which means that a seed will be fertile for only one season, thus stopping the usual collection and subsequent replanting of seeds by farmers for the next harvest. Such collecting has been specifically excluded in Monsanto's three-year contracts for supplying canola (rape seed) in North America.[51]

These companies have undeniably been very clever in their learning. But all learning has a moral dimension. Is this learning being used wisely? As Shell learned so painfully from their Brent Spar débâcle, no matter how apparently reliable the science and the logic of the argument, it is the public's perception of, and emotional reaction to, the issue that will eventually determine the outcome. As I write, Deutsche Bank analysts have announced GM foods 'dead' as a European investment opportunity, and US manufacturers are bowing to pressure in North America by stopping mixing GM with other grains to allow farmers a choice of whether or not to use GM seeds. Time will tell as to the outcome, but there will be a lot more learning to do by both sides before the values, acceptable behaviours, and consequences of investing in learning to create such assets are understood fully.

There is a deeper moral argument here which reflects the conflict between the scientific and the commercial values of learning. When the Utah University team 'discovered' nuclear 'cold' fusion they did not do what academic values and protocols have traditionally demanded – publishing quickly in a refereed journal like *Nature* – to share their breakthrough with the international scholastic community. Instead they sought out the US Patent Office to protect 'their' intellectual property. If such commercially-orientated behaviour begins to set a new value for science, then we are likely to lose effective scholarship and ultimately academic freedom. If corporations, including universities, first seek to protect their investment, and only then sell on their learning at prices they will determine, then the obvious benefits of organizational learning in creating a civil society may become soured.

The 'shadow side' of the development of intellectual property is also seen in the present argument over alleged 'bio- piracy' by pharmaceutical and bio-science companies. Many are trying to establish intellectual property rights over naturally occurring substances. So their exploration and codification of, for example, the diversity of plants in the rainforests, and traditional herbal medicines, is leading many local communities in the developing countries to cry foul. They argue that the creation of any form of intellectual property rights over such natural substances, or their derivatives, may cripple their culture and their economy. As I have said, all learning has a moral dimension.

The growing push in advanced economies for the establishment and monopolization of intellectual property rights will not go away although the Internet may help diffuse some of the worst consequences. The intellectual property acquisition process will increase significantly as the twenty-first century unfolds. Performance-orientated learning boards will need to accept both the positive, and negative, aspects of the growth in intellectual property rights and then combine this knowledge with continuous learning and critical debate, for their organizations. The careful positioning of the board at the strategic centre of the three learning cycles will increase their organization's ability to learn, adapt and create these 'learning assets' more democratically and more rapidly in an increasingly complex world. Sadly most organizations do not know what their people have already learned. The adoption by the board and senior executives of regular intellectual property audits will be a necessary step towards the Learning Organization.

## CORPORATE MEMORY AND CORPORATE AMNESIA

> She wondered if there was such a thing as collective memory,
> something more than the sum of individual memories. If so,
> was it coterminous, yet in some way richer; or did it last
> longer? She wondered if those too young to have original
> knowledge could be given memory, could have it grafted on?
> Julian Barnes[52]

A few organizations are to be praised for taking a more strategic
look at both their acquisition, and loss, of organizational learning.
How can a twenty-year-old bank clerk be expected to effectively
'manage' a branch or 'service centre' without access to long-term
experience? I realize that such people are seen by many executives
as cheap and expendable, but if by employing them you give a
strong message to your customers that customer service is not
important, then what does this do for mid to long-term shareholder value?

Moreover, if you sack all staff aged over fifty 'because they and
their pensions are too expensive' then what happens to them and
their accumulated learning? It vaporizes with their departure and
you are left with a less experienced and less connected organization. An extreme example in the UK is seen in the privatization
of British Rail. The privatization was not the sell-off and transfer
of a single organization, but a politically expedient decision to
fragment the old system into four component parts – track, rolling
stock, maintenance, and train operators. In turn each of these
were fragmented into a total of 100 privatized companies. The
potential for a massive loss of learning, and the alienation of
customers and staff, is huge.

And so it has turned out to be. While the shareholders are being
well-served, and customer numbers rise, complaints have risen
exponentially as delays and cancellations also rise. Many of these
problems are due to the non-integration and the lack of a learning
culture in the new rail 'system'. There is no incentive for the
dominant operator, Railtrack, which owns the track, signals and
buildings, to invest. This is made worse by the shortness of the

most train operating companies' contracts, often just seven years, encouraging everyone to take a short-term 'bottom-line' view because they have little certainty about having a mid to long-term future. This leads to a very good example of a large-scale 'blame culture' in action.

All elements of the system are penalized if they do not meet legally specified (low) performance indicators. So it pays to blame others and fiddle performance indicators. This absorbs a large amount of organizational time, energy and money so the customer perspective is easily lost. Matters are made worse by the sacking of many older, experienced, personnel to avoid paying higher salaries and pensions. This drains away the 'know-how' and 'know-why' of each organization, and the ability to integrate the total system. Much of this learning was never fully codified and diffused under British Rail. It resided in the heads and hands of the staff. This leaves dangerous gaps in the new rail system. Already the loss of such learning has been implicated in some accidents like Bromley and Southall, and has the potential to cause many more. The political decision by the Conservative government to rush through the privatization before an election has left the next generation with a more complex and disintegrated transport problem which the privatization was meant to resolve.

The blame culture resulting from the Paddington rail tragedy in 1999 was appalling to witness. The only good that may emerge is the heightened public awareness of the many problems with the UK's railways governance, and the likely highlighting of the real seats of blame through a public enquiry. Significantly, just a few weeks later a second UK precedent was created by a court on the vexed issue of corporate manslaughter, when the managing director of a haulage firm was jailed for encouraging his drivers to work over-long hours and to disconnect their tachographs.

All boards of directors, and senior executives, have a key role in protecting and developing the 'corporate memory' on both the 'hard', intellectual property generation, side and the 'soft' vision, culture and values and behaviours side. If they neglect this, then they risk 'corporate amnesia'. Arnold Kransdorff's book *Corporate Amnesia*[53] gives excellent examples of organizations failing to codify and diffuse their learning, so that they are forced to use, or abuse, their scarce resources to keep re-learning that in which they have already invested. At their best they are merely 'Bourbon organizations' which seem to learn nothing, and forget nothing. At their worst they have not learned that history repeats itself first as tragedy, then as farce.

## Developing democracy in organizations

Learning Organizations are designed to combat such tragic and farcical organizations. It is only through the democratizing of work processes by sharing information more transparently, acting more honestly and being comfortable with your accountability through participation and informed choices, that sufficient learning will be generated to ensure that an organization's rate of learning is equal to, or greater than, the rate of change in its environment.

In Figure 23 I have listed some of the many, often unco-ordinated, approaches happening at operational, strategy and policy levels of organizations for improving organizational effectiveness and efficiency. Like it or not (and many directors and managers do not), these are driving organizations towards a more democratic approach to people at work. The rapid rise of 360 degree appraisal alone is a highly democratizing force at the operational level through its opening up of the transparency of the organization's assessment and rewards processes and the clarification of its values. The more sensitive handling of customers' immediate and latent needs, and the development of the 'triple bottom-line' approach are good examples of the gradual democratization of Policy Learning. And the use of more 'town meetings', action learning groups and critical review debates opens the learning board to higher quality risk-assessment and decision-taking for Strategic Learning – to the benefit of the organization and its stakeholders alike.

There is no simple macro-political imperative which is driving the democratization of organizations – much of it is unwitting and unfocused in terms of the bigger picture. It is happening fragmentedly. But it is happening because we are having to learn

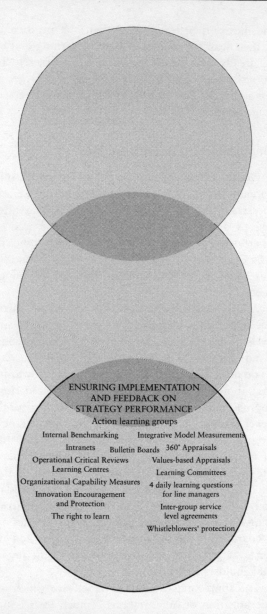

**Figure 23(a) The Operational Learning Cycle. The learning processes forcing the democratization of organizations**

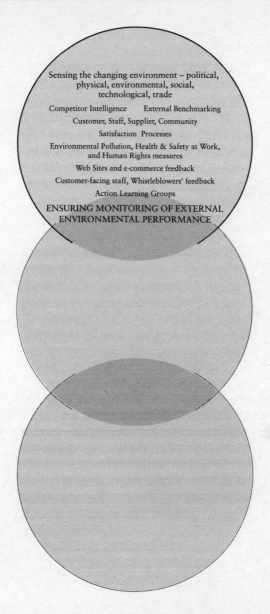

Sensing the changing environment – political, physical, environmental, social, technological, trade

Competitor Intelligence        External Benchmarking

Customer, Staff, Supplier, Community

Satisfaction  Processes

Environmental Pollution, Health & Safety at Work, and Human Rights measures

Web Sites and e-commerce feedback

Customer-facing staff, Whistleblowers' feedback

Action Learning Groups

ENSURING MONITORING OF EXTERNAL ENVIRONMENTAL PERFORMANCE

Figure 23(b) The Policy Learning Cycle. The growing democratization processes in a Learning Organization

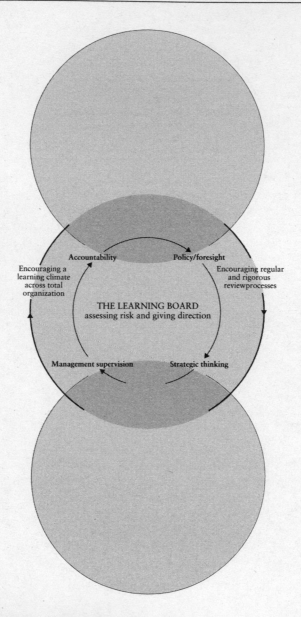

**Figure 23(c) Strategic Learning Cycle**

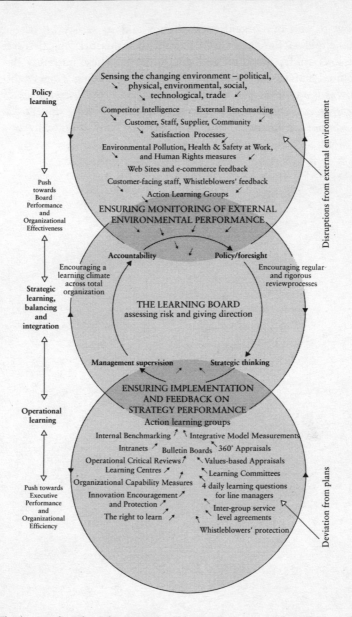

**Figure 23(d) The Three Cycles of Learning**

how to run our organizations better and so satisfy *all* of our stakeholders simultaneously. I think that this drawing deserves serious study, reflection and development. These currently disjointed activities and learning processes are leading us inevitably towards a time when the *'individual and collective learning which reinforces the informed, conscious and discriminating choices that underpin democracy'* becomes a reality. Now that really is a vision!

# A Personal History of the Development of the Learning Organization Concept

Despite popular belief the Learning Organization idea did not start in the UK or US in the 1980s. It has moral and scientific roots which go back deep into history. By the end of the Second World War the work of Reg Revans, Fritz Schumacher, and Jacob Bronowski under the supervision of Sir Geoffrey Vickers formed the Intelligence Unit of the newly nationalized National Coal Board in the UK. They created at individual, workgroup and organizational levels a system of 'action learning' processes – the engine that drives the Learning Organization. Their design for dynamic learning processes was influenced also by a fundamental rethinking of economics which led later to the publication of the influential text *Small is Beautiful*[54]. Their use of small self-managing groups, the rigorous collection of statistical data and the power generated by tapping the group's positive energies for and commitment to change was not recognized at the time as the intellectual breakthrough in organizational learning, thought and practice that it was. Similar processes were developed, but in a more limited way, by Juran and Deming's work on quality assurance and statistical methods in Japan during the late 1940s. Whereas Revans' work led to 'learning circles' the Japanese Productivity Council, allied to Juran and Deming's work, led to the explosive development of 'quality circles'.

Fundamental to such thinking was the idea that the application of the scientific process – of careful observation, reflection, the creation of a hypothesis, careful experimentation, reflection leading to action, feedback, codification and rapid diffusion of the results – was the key to understanding organizational learning. As they moved into the early 1950s organizational theorists were able to call on complementary disciplines to back up their work, especially 'systems thinking' particularly Ashby's thoughts on the need for sufficient diversity[55] – and the Tavistock Institute's pioneering work on 'socio-technical systems'[56].

This promising start was followed in the 1960s and 1970s by a surprisingly fallow period for the development of organizational learning ideas. This coincided with the rise of the inaptly named 'scientific management' school of academics and consultants who became dominant in US and UK business and in the emerging business schools. These thrived on a more 'Newtonian' notion of a fixed universe with immutable laws within which all human problems were reduced to a single answer through the application of logic and rationality and with the answer being delivered in almost exclusively financial terms. The rise of 'rationalist' managers and accountants unbalanced (in a dangerously negative way) our notions of what constitutes a healthy human organization. In the US only the humanistic psychologists, particularly Abraham Maslow, David McGregor, Carl Rogers and Roger Harrison and later Charles Hampden-Turner, kept the flag flying. They were supported by the cybernetician Norbert Wiener whose influential book *The Human Use of Human Beings*[57] remains a classic.

The two new UK business schools at London and Manchester were strongly influenced by US rationalist ideology but the dominance of this was tempered by the appointment of more holistic and humane thinkers about organizations. Included in this list of honour are Reg Revans, Charles Handy, John Morris, Tom Lupton, and Stafford Beer. As an aside it was Charles Handy and John Morris who encouraged my move from architecture and community development education into the world of organizations and business.

These people pursued in their different ways the importance of learning as a central organizational process, and of the need for a series of integrated levels of learning in any healthy organization.

The earliest and clearest model was Revans' 'systems Alpha, Beta and Gamma'[58] although many did not recognize this at the time, not least because he was working outside the US/UK academic world in Belgium. His return to prominence in the UK was aided by Lord Weinstock at the General Electric Company (GEC) in 1974. Revans was asked to design and launch the *GEC Developing Senior Managers Programme*. A team of action learning facilitators led by Jean Lawrence and David Casey and including David Sutton, Alan Lawlor, Tony Eccles, Ian Cunningham and myself was brought in. They were supported inside the GEC by Mike Bett, David Pearce, Geoff Gaines, John Shrigley, Hugh Allen and Glynn Trollope. Over the next five years this team had a major effect on the UK's understanding of how beneficial action learning processes could be for an organization. This was a defining moment for establishing the credibility of organizational learning as a business tool.

By the late 1970s action learning ideas were evolving within and between groups of enthusiasts especially in the UK and the 'Learning Organization' movement began to pick up speed. My colleague Tony Hodgson and I worked informally on the dynamic interplay of learning at the policy, strategy, and operational levels which led later to my 'triple-loop learning' model of the Learning Organization which became the basis for the original version of this book.[59] Similar notions of interacting levels of organizational learning were developing in the US with the work of Weick, with Watzlawick, Weakland and Fisch with their book *Change: Principles of Problem Formation and Problem Resolution*[60] and with Chris Argyris, whose work became highly influential in the design of Learning Organizations through his ideas on 'double-loop learning'.[61] In the UK, the work of the 'Trans-Pennine group', especially Mike Pedler, Tom Boydell, Malcolm Leary, John Burgoyne and David Megginson and the emergence of the Learning Company model further developed the credibility of organizational learning in both practice and academia.

Peter Senge's internationally influential *The Fifth Discipline*[62] published at the start of the 1990s gave the Learning Organization movement massive publicity and reinforced the notion of systems thinking as an important component to organizational learning, reflecting the work of Norbert Wiener nearly forty years before. Many new publications expanded this theme, including the work of David Garvey, Arie de Geus's *The Living Company*,[63] the work on 'dilemmas' by Charles Hampden-Turner and Fons Trompenaars[64], Max Boisot's *Knowledge Assets*[65], and my own work on 'the Learning Board' as the central integrator and processor of the Learning Organization – published in *The Fish Rots from the Head*.[66] As new work on complexity theory is put forward (especially from the Santa Fe Institute) we come up-to-date with this personal history of the progression of the idea of the Learning Organization.

For me the most exciting development at present has been the spontaneous coming together of a number of people long-experienced in learning processes. This group, convened originally by Michael Pearn, includes; Peter Honey, Alan Mumford (whose work on *The Learning Styles Inventory* has been of great help to me), John Burgoyne, Ian Cunningham, Mike Pedler, Andrew Mayo and myself. Margaret Attwood, Tom Boydell, David Clutterbuck, David Megginson and Robin Wood have now joined us. Our informal discussions led to the *Declaration on Learning* in 1998 and evolved into *The Learning Symposium* and a revised *Declaration* (*www.peterhoneylearning.com*). This is influencing policy-makers on national and international issues of continuous learning. We are especially concerned with readjusting the present personal/state balance in learning provision in favour of the individual.

By definition organizational learning is a dynamic process in which ideas will keep evolving. Complexity theory and the impact of the Internet – particularly e-commerce – will lead us into the next millennium. The advances in digital information management systems pose us great opportunities to encourage more rigorous organizational learning, as shown in Bill Gates' book *Business @ the Speed Of Thought*[67]. His central thesis is the importance of the 'digital nervous system' of an organization and is, if you strip out the word 'digital', little different from what Revans and his colleagues were advocating back in the 1940s. However the technology to achieve it is now much more effective. The crucial questions are still: do we have the imagination and values to commit to true organizational learning; and will we be willing to transfer sufficient power within and between organizations to do this democratically?

# Acknowledgements

I would like to thank Lucinda McNeile, Tamsin Miller, Sarah Hodgson and Sally Garratt for the great support I was given in the massive revision of this book; and to Margarete Hult for the use, yet again, of Villa Gabrielle, Tourette-sur-Loup, France in which to write it in peace.

# Notes

1. *A Declaration on Learning*, J. Burgoyne, I. Cunningham, R. Garratt, P. Honey, A. Mayo, A. Mumford, M. Pearn & M. Pedler, (Peter Honey Publications, 1998).
2. *The Strategy Safari*, H. Mintzberg, J. Lampel, B. Anisbrand, (Jossey-Bass Inc., 1998).
3. Institute of Directors, Chartered Director Initiative. Institute of Directors, 116 Pall Mall, London SW1, UK.
4. *Knowledge Assets*, M. Boisot, (Oxford University Press, 1998).
5. *Cannibals with Forks*, J. Elkington, (New Society Publishers, 1998).
6. *The Origins and Growth of Action Learning*, R. W. Revans, Chartwell-Bratt, Bromley and Lund, 1982.
7. Learning Board model R. Garratt *The Fish Rots from the Head: The Crisis in our Boardrooms* (HarperCollinsBusiness, 1995).
8. PIMS.
9. D. Lane, Santa Fe Institute, California, US, 1997.
10. *Co-opetition*, A. Brandenberger & B. Nalebuff (HarperCollinsBusiness, 1996).
11. *Moments of Truth*, J. Carlzon & T. Peters (Ballinger, Cambridge, 1989).
12. *ABC of Action Learning*, R. W. Revans (Lemon & Crane, 1998).
13. C. Sworder 'Hearing the baby's cry: it's all in the thinking,' in *Developing Strategic Thought*, ed. R. Garratt, (HarperCollins, 1996).
14. *Change: Problem Formation and Problem Resolution*, P. Watzlawick, J. Weakland, & R. Fisch, (W. W. Norton, 1974).

15. *Knowledge for Action*, C. Argyris, (Jossey-Bass, 1993).
16. *The Rise and Fall of Strategic Planning*, H. Mintzberg, (Prentice Hall, Europe, 1993).
17. *Corporate Strategy*, I. Ansoff (Penguin, 1988).
18. *Business @ the Speed of Thought*, W. Gates (Penguin, 1999).
19. J. Browne, 'Unleashing the power of learning,' in *Harvard Business Review*, Sept–Oct 1997.
20. *The Twelve Organizational Capabilities*, R. Garratt, (HarperCollinsBusiness, 2000).
21. *Corporate Collapse*, J. Argenti (McGraw-Hill, 1973).
22. J. Morris, 'Good Company' in *Management Education & Development*, vol 18 Part 2, 103–115 (1987).
23. Institute of Directors, 116 Pall Mall, London SW1, UK.
24. *The Service Profit Chain*, J. L. Heskett, W. Sasser & L. Schlesiger, (Free Press, 1997).
25. R. Garratt, op. cit.
26. P. Smith 'Stages of a Manager's Job' in *Current Research in Management*, ed. V. Hammond (Frances Pinter Publishers, 1982).
27. *Moments of Truth*, J. Carlzon & T. Peters (HarperCollins, 1989).
28. J. Browne, Unleashing the power of learning,' in *Harvard Business Review*.
29. *ABC of Action Learning*, R. Revans, (Lemos & Crane, 1998).
30. Turnbull Report, Institute of Chartered Accountants, London, 1999.
31. Streamline, ibid.
32. *The Importance of Cultures*, C. Geertz (Basic Books, 1973).
33. *Cannibals with Forks*, J. Elkington, (New Society Publishers, 1998).
34. Learning Board model, R. Garratt, op. cit.
35. Modified IOD dilemmas from *Standards for the Board*, Institute of Directors, London.
36. *The Rise and Fall of Strategic Planning*, H. Mintzberg, (Prentice Hall, Europe, 1993).
37. I. Ansoff op. cit.
38. H. Mintzberg 'Strategic thinking as seeing,' in *Developing Strategic Thought*, ed. R. Garratt, (HarperCollins, 1996).

39. Jerry Rhodes, Cotswold House, 16 Bradley Street, Wotton-under-Edge, Gloucestershire, UK.

40. Thinking Intentions Profile.

41. *The Fish Rots from the Head*, R. Garratt (HarperCollins-Business, 1996).

42. *Developing Strategic Thought*, ed. R. Garratt (HarperCollins-Business, 1995).

43. A. Brandenberger & B. Nalebuff op. cit.

44. *Competitive Advantage*, M. Porter (Free Press, 1980).

45. *Competitive Strategy*, M. Porter (Free Press, 1983).

46. Booz Allen/*The Economist* Report.

47. European Foundation for Quality Management – 'Business excellence model'. Details can be obtained from the British Quality Foundation, 32 Great Peter Street, London, (UK) SW1. Telephone 0207 654 5000.

48. *The Balanced Scorecard*, R. S. Kaplan & P. Norton, (Harvard Business School Press, 1996).

49. *The Modern Corporation and Private Property*, A. A. Berle & G. C.Means (Transaction Publishers, 1991).

50. M. Boisot, op. cit.

51. *Financial Times*, 13 July, 1999.

52. J. Barnes, 'Evermore' in *Cross Channel*, J. Barnes (Jonathan Cape, 1996).

53. *Corporate Amnesia*, A. Kransdorff (Butterworth-Heinemann, 1998).

54. *Small is Beautiful*, E. F. Schumacher (Vintage, 1993).

55. Ashby – sufficient diversity: 'Self Regulation and Requisite Variety' in *Introduction to Cybernetics* (Wiley, 1956).

56. Tavistock – socio tech systems: 'Exforces in Groups' in *Human Relations* vol Part IV, (Tavistock Publications, 1948).

57. *The Human Use of Human Beings*, N. Wiener (Free Association Books, 1989).

58. Revans, op. cit.

59. *The Learning Organization*, R. Garratt, (Fontana, 1987).

60. P. Watzlawick, J. Weakland, & R. Fisch, op. cit.

61. *Organizational Learning*, C. Argyris, (Addison Wesley, 1978).

62. *The Fifth Discipline*, P. Senge (Century/Arrow, 1996).

63. *The Living Company*, A. de Geus (Nicholas Brealey Publishing, 1999).
64. *Riding the Wave of Culture*, C. Hampden-Turner & F. Trompenaars (Nicholas Brealey Publishing, 1993).
65. M. Boisot, op. cit.
66. R. Garratt, op. cit.
67. W. Gates, op. cit.

# Index

Figures in bold type refer to diagrams